Linux for Windows users

Other Computer Tiles

by

R.A.Penfold

BP450 How to Expand and Upgrade Your PC
BP467 How to Interface PCs
BP479 How to Build Your Own PC

Linux for Windows users

R.A.Penfold

Bernard Babani (publishing) Ltd
The Grampians
Shepherds Bush Road
London W6 7NF
England

Please Note

First Published – October 1999
Reprinted – October 2000

British Library Cataloguing in Publication Data
A catalogue record for this book is available from the British Library

ISBN 0 85934 470 3

Cover Design by Gregor Arthur
Printed and bound in Great Britain by Cox & Wyman Ltd, Reading

Preface

Although once strictly for the knowledgeable enthusiast or computing professional, the Linux operating system has rapidly moved into the mainstream and now offers a real alternative to the operating systems from the major corporations. Undoubtedly a big attraction of this operating system is that it is free. It can actually be bought in several distributions as either a set of CD-ROMs or CD-ROMs plus printed manuals, but it can also be downloaded free from the Internet. Probably most new users now obtain Linux in the form of a "free" CD-ROM given away with a computer magazine. In addition to the operating system there are usually countless utilities and applications programs included on most Linux CD-ROMs. In the computing value for money stakes it has few rivals.

It is not necessary to have a PC especially for Linux, and provided there is sufficient hard disc space it can coexist with another operating system using a dual-boot system. As most Linux software will run quite happily on something considerably less than the latest wonder PC, Linux can be used to give an old and otherwise unused PC a new lease of life. Linux tends to be associated with large networks, but it will function perfectly well as the operating system for a workstation. It is increasing used in this way, and in this publication only its use with workstations is covered.

On the face of it Linux is not all that different to Windows, offering a command line interface similar to MS/DOS and a graphical user interface (GUI). There are some major differences though, and even the most accomplished of Windows users can have problems getting started with Linux. Unless you know how, even getting *in* to Linux in the first place can be difficult! Many Linux publications get bogged down in the history of this operating system, technicalities that are (initially anyway) irrelevant to most users, and arcane commands that are of little use to most current users. This book takes the "cut to the chase" approach, concentrating on everyday computing with Linux. You do not have to be an expert to use a Windows system, and few of the many Windows users have more than a cursory understanding of the subject. The same is true with Linux, and it is not necessary to have an in-depth understanding of it in order to run programs, copy and delete files, etc. You can learn to use the system first, and learn about the technicalities later, as and when it becomes necessary.

Where possible the conversion from Windows to Linux is made as "painless" as possible by drawing parallels between the two systems. It is assumed that the reader has a basic working knowledge of MS/DOS and Windows, but no more than this. In order to follow the material pertaining to the command line interpreter any moderately recent version of Linux should suffice. There is more than one GUI available for Linux, but the K Desktop Environment (KDE) is the most widely used and is now included with all the major Linux distributions. To utilize the GUI material KDE version 1.0 will suffice, but you should preferably use version 1.1 or later.

R.A.Penfold

Contents

1

3

4

Also need to know 115

Trademarks

MS/DOS, Windows 95, Windows 98, and Windows NT are registered trademarks of Microsoft Corporation

Partition Magic and Boot Magic are registered trademarks of PowerQuest Corporation

WordPerfect is a registered trademark of Corel Corporation

Star Office is a registered trademark of StarDivision Corporation

PostScript is a registered trademark of Adobe Systems Incorporated

1

Installation

Spoilt for choice

One slightly confusing aspect for the newcomer to Linux is that several different software houses produce it. To understand how this has come about we need to briefly examine the origins of Linux. Linux was produced by a group of individuals, led by Linus Torvalds, trying to write a version of the UNIX operating system for computers having Intel processors. In practice this effectively meant producing a version of UNIX for IBM PCs and compatibles, although there are some other computers based on Intel processors. UNIX is widely regarded as one of the most powerful and versatile operating systems available, and it is commonly encountered on high-end workstations, particularly those used in scientific and technical applications. It is also used as the operating system for computer networks of course. A group of people working via the Internet to produce something as complex as a UNIX style operating system may seem to be a bit over-ambitious, but the project was successful, and has continued to blossom.

So what features does Linux offer, and who needs them? It has to be admitted that Linux is probably over-specified for many users. This is not necessarily a drawback, since you can simply ignore any features that you do not require. They are still there if you should need them at some later date.

Multitasking

Linux has full multitasking capability, and will happily run umpteen programs simultaneously if the hardware is up to the task.

Multi-user

It is also able to support multiple users concurrently. This is really only of consequence when Linux is used in a computer network, which is something it handles very well. However, here we are only concerned with Linux as the operating system for workstations, and concurrent multi-user operation is something that will not be considered further.

Non-concurrent

Linux also has facilities for non-concurrent multi-user operation, where operators use the computer one at a time. To each operator or group of operators it appears as though they have their own computer with no other users.

Security

As a byproduct of its multi-user capability Linux has good security features. Each user has his or her own password, and can have files that are not accessible by other users. There is a separate password for the system supervisor or administrator, and most changes to the system can only be implemented by logging in as the supervisor. This should ensure that inexperienced users do not accidentally make changes to the system set-up that would be difficult to correct. These security features are clearly very useful where a computer will be used by more than one person, but even for a single user they make it more difficult for anyone who tries to access or tamper with your data files.

Source code

Linux is often referred to as a free operating system, but this word is a bit ambiguous in a Linux context. It is often used in the free-speech meaning of the word rather than the free lunch meaning. Most non-Linux software is sold on an as-is basis, and if it is has minor bugs there is nothing you can do except complain and hope that a suitable fix turns up in due course. If you do not like certain aspects of the way in which the software operates there is usually no way of altering them, even if minor tweaks to the program code are all that is required. Linux is much more accommodating in that it is supplied complete with the source code, and so is much Linux utility and application software. In theory at any rate, you can alter the source code and recompile the programs in order to tailor them to your exact requirements, or to remove any bugs that you might encounter. In reality this sort of thing is well beyond the capabilities of most users, and hiring someone to do the job for you is likely to be prohibitively expensive. On the other hand, the Linux community has plenty of users who are prepared to use their expertise to help others for little or no remuneration.

It is free

No doubt a big attraction of Linux for many is that it is also free in the free lunch sense. It can be downloaded from the Internet, although obtaining a reasonably full implementation of Linux in this way is likely to be very time consuming, even if you have a fast Internet connection. It would probably take several days if you do not! From time to time computer magazines come complete with Linux on a "free" CD-ROM, and this probably represents the best way to try out Linux at minimal cost. The third option is to buy Linux, which is where things can get a little confusing. There are several versions available, and in some cases more than one version of each version.

Versions

Although Linux has a lot in its favour, there is one major drawback, and it is this that has resulted in various versions of Linux becoming available. Linux is a very powerful 32-bit operating system, but in its most basic usable form it does not have a graphical user interface (GUI). Commands are entered into a command line editor, and when used in this way it could be regarded as a sort of turbocharged MS/DOS. Also, in its raw state it can be very difficult to get Linux installed properly. This has led to various individuals and companies producing Linux enhancements that make it easier to use and (or) install. Whatever your source for Linux, you are unlikely to get just the Linux kernel. With a magazine version you will normally get one CD-ROM containing the Linux kernel and various support files, a program or programs to take you through the installation process and make things as easy as possible, plus what is like to be dozens of utility and applications programs. There should also be a fair amount of documentation included on the disc, and possibly some source code.

If you buy Linux you will generally get more in the way of utilities and applications programs, plus more on-disc documentation. The quantity of material is such that a single CD-ROM is insufficient, and there are typically two to four CD-ROMs in a Linux set. With the cheaper versions there will be little or no printed manuals, but the more expensive implementations are supplied with a large amount of printed documentation. If you download Linux over the Internet or obtain it free with a computer magazine you are more or less on your own, and can not reasonably expect to receive much in the way of technical support. This is not necessarily that important, since there are many sources of help available if you have an Internet connection. If you buy Linux there should at least be free technical support for a limited period to help you get everything installed correctly.

Newcomers to Linux often query the fact that you can buy this supposedly free operating system, and that some implementations are not particularly cheap. What you are paying for is the CD-ROMs themselves rather than the software that they contain. You are also paying for any printed manuals and technical support. In some cases you may also be paying for software included on the CD-ROMs that is not free. As with most things in life, you tend to get what you pay for. The more you pay, the more printed manuals, technical support, etc., you are likely to get. You have to decide for yourself whether the extras are worth paying for.

Distributions

There are four main versions of Linux, or distributions as they are called in the generally accepted terminology. Any of these will provide you with a good usable Linux installation, and make the installation process reasonably hassle free. Here are brief details of each distribution.

Red Hat

The Red Hat distribution is almost certainly the most popular, and this is the big name in the Linux world. Red Hat has received funding from large companies such as Intel, which should enable it to develop Linux more rapidly. Red Hat developments include the GNOME graphical user interface and the RPM (Red Hat Package Manager) software installation system. I suppose this has to be considered the "safe" option, since most Linux software will run under a recent version of this distribution. It is also quite easy to install Red Hat Linux.

Caldera

There are actually two distributions of Caldera Open Linux, which are the normal and "Lite" versions. The standard distribution is aimed at corporate users, and due to its commercial content is not freely distributable. Open Linux Lite lacks the commercial software and can be freely distributed. Until recently neither version was widely available in the UK, but the full version now seems to be readily available. It is supplied complete with the KDE graphical user interface, and in recent versions KDE forms a central part of the system. Caldera Open Linux is reasonably straightforward to install and use, and in the latest versions it can be easily installed alongside Windows in a dual boot set-up. For a first-time user it is quite a good choice.

Slackware

This is one of the oldest distributions, and is felt by some to be less go ahead than the other main distributions. It is a good usable version of

Linux though, and it is reasonably easy to install. It is readily available in the UK, and is available quite cheaply if you will settle for the CDs with no printed manuals.

SuSE

The other three distributions originate in the USA, but SuSE Linux comes from Germany. It has become quite popular in Europe, including the UK where it is readily available. It is apparently less easy to obtain than the other three distributions outside Europe. This is an up to the minute distribution that comes complete with the KDE graphical user interface. I have sometimes found SuSE Linux a little awkward to get up and running, but with a little determination beginners should be able to get it working properly. Updates of the English language version tend to lag slightly behind the German version.

There are actually a number of other distributions, such as Debian and Turbo Linux, but these would seem to be less widely available in the UK than the four distributions listed above. For newcomers it is probably best to use one of the main distributions, and any of them should give good stable results.

The numbers game

With most operating systems new versions are few and far between. I have one PC, which is now several years old, and nearing the end of its useful operating life, but with the aid of five updates via service packs its operating system is still the current version. Things are different with Linux, where there seems to be a constant stream of new versions. This is the case with the kernel itself, and with the various distributions. A Linux kernel has a type number along the lines 2.2.4. The first number indicates the major version number, and changes very infrequently indeed. The second digit is the minor version number, and this changes much more frequently. The final number is the revision number, which changes every few months, or less. It is best to avoid odd numbered minor version numbers as these are development kernels, or what would be considered beta code in normal computing terms. Kernels of this type are not supplied with the main Linux distributions. At the time of writing this, the most up-to-date minor version is version 2, but this has not yet found its way into all the main distributions.

Linux distributions normally have two digit version numbers such as 5.3 or 6.0, much like most Windows software. The second digit is likely to change about twice per year, with the first digit changing about every two years when there is some major change. If you have a version of Linux that is a decimal point or two behind the current version it is not completely up-to-date, but on the other hand it is not really out of date either.

Hardware

Linux is a powerful 32-bit operating system, so do you need a powerful PC in order to run it properly? This is a "how long is a piece of string" style question and the hardware requirements depend on the applications software you intend to use. It also depends on whether you require a "bare bones" Linux installation or an "all-singing all-dancing" version. The absolute minimum needed to run Linux is a PC having an 80386 microprocessor, about 8 MB of memory, approximately 54 MB of hard disk space, a mouse, supported video card, and a CD-ROM drive. Although a PC version of Linux will run on a computer as basic as this, it would be misleading to suggest that this is all you need to run Linux effectively.

Hard drive

The basic Linux operating system uses a command line interpreter where you type in commands, much like using MS/DOS. To fully utilize this operating system you really need to install the X Windows, which roughly doubles the amount of hard disc space required. It is also advantageous to set aside some disc space for use as a swap file. This is space that the operating system will use for temporary file storage, and up to 100 MB can be used. The swap space is normally at least equal to the amount of memory fitted to the computer. Last, and by no means least, you will need some disc space for applications and utility software. Even a version of Linux supplied on a single CD-ROM will come complete will many megabytes of useful utilities and some applications software, and you will no doubt wish to add more software over a period of time. A typical Linux installation takes up about 350 to 450 MB initially, plus the space for a swap file. Do not forget that you will also need some space for your data files. Realistically, a minimum of something like a 540 MB hard drive is needed for a reasonably full and effective installation. 850 MB or more is preferable.

Processor

Although Linux tends to be less demanding on the processor than many other operating systems, it would be unrealistic to load it onto an old 33 MHz 80386 based PC and expect it to run like the latest Pentium wonder computers. If you are going to use X Windows and some of the more powerful applications programs you will require at least a fast 80486-based PC, and preferably some sort of Pentium based PC. Obviously some software may require a more potent processor, but for most purposes something like a 100 to 200 MHz Pentium processor is adequate.

Memory

Although 8 MB of memory should be sufficient to get Linux "up and running", it is definitely preferable to have more than this. You could probably get by quite well with 16 MB, but everything is likely to run faster and more smoothly with 32 MB or more. Some of the more advanced applications programs require a minimum of 32 MB. As memory is quite cheap these days it does not really make sense to skimp on memory, and if necessary it would be well worthwhile investing in a memory upgrade. This leaves plenty of "headroom" if you need to do multitasking.

CD-ROM

It is possible to install some older versions of Linux from floppy discs, but modern distributions are supplied on one or more CD-ROMs, and you will therefore need some sort of CD-ROM drive. Installation is much quicker using a fast drive, but something like an old 2X drive will suffice. A CD-ROM drive using an ordinary ATAPI (IDE) interface should give no problems, but some SCSII drives might not be supported. The more common the hardware in your computer, the better the chances of getting it to work well with Linux.

Pointing devices

Practically any mouse should be suitable, and Linux supports serial, bus, and mouse port mice. In theory a three-button mouse is required, but a two-button mouse can provide an emulation of the three-button type. Pressing both buttons simulates pressing the middle mouse button. In practice little modern Linux software is actually reliant on the third button. If you should have problems getting Linux to operate with the mouse, a Microsoft compatible mouse can be purchased for next to nothing these days, so this is not really a major problem. One drawback of Linux is that it lacks in-depth hardware support. If you wish to use a graphics tablet or some other exotic form of pointing device you may find that it will not work with Linux.

Graphics card

The same is true of some graphics cards. There tends to be a lag between a new video chipset being produced and the Linux drivers for the chipset being released. With the less popular chipsets there is no guarantee that suitable drivers will ever be produced. If your PC is fitted with the very latest 3D-video wonder board with all the latest go faster facilities it may be a while before it can be used with Linux as anything other than a straightforward VGA card. Any mainstream graphics board that has been around for at least a few months is likely to be supported. If the present card is not supported, fitting something like a S3 based board or an ATI board built around one of the Rage II series of chips should cost very little.

Monitor

A standard VGA monitor having a resolution of 640 by 480 pixels is the minimum requirement, but if you intend to use X Windows higher resolution is preferable. You may have the option of using a virtual screen where the main window has a resolution of (say) 1024 by 768 pixels, but the monitor only shows 640 by 480 pixels at any one time. You can scroll around the screen to display the area of interest. In practice I have found this type of thing to be a little awkward, and where possible it is better to use the screen at a higher resolution of 800 by 600 or 1024 by 768 pixels. Even if it results in rather small menu text, etc., on the screen, I would still recommend using the monitor at one of these higher resolutions.

In the final analysis the only way to determine whether or not your PC's hardware is compatible with Linux is the "suck it and see" approach. If there is no specific support for the video card or mouse it may well be that there is support for a compatible device, and using the driver for this device will give satisfactory results. With a video card it is worth studying the instruction manual to determine the chipset it uses. Alternatively, try looking at the chips on the card itself. Using the driver for a board that uses the same chipset as your video card will often produce satisfactory results.

Unless you are going to use some particularly demanding software it is not necessary to have the latest "state of the art" PC. After upgrading to a new PC many users would like to put their old PC to good use, particularly if it is not that old and has plenty of life left in it. A PC that will not work very well with most other operating systems may well produce perfectly good results when used with Linux. This factor is probably a major cause of the sudden increase in the popularity of Linux. Rather than disposing of an old PC it can be given a new least of life by using it as a Linux workstation. If you are buying a PC specifically to give Linux a try it is not necessary to opt for a highly specified and expensive PC. Indeed, unless you are going to use some demanding software a good second-hand PC is all that is needed. The current low cost of new PCs has forced second-hand prices down to the point where even some quite recent PCs are on offer at bargain basement prices. Whether you buy a new or pre-used PC, in order to avoid compatibility problems it is advisable to choose one that has "middle of the road" drives, graphics card, etc.

Peripherals

Assuming that Linux will work properly with your PC, will it also operate with peripherals such as printers and modems? This very much depends on the particular peripherals you are using, and the more common the device, the better the chance of it being supported by Linux. If you can not find specific support for a printer or other peripheral it is possible that drivers for a compatible device are included. For example, many laser printers have a mode where they emulate a Hewlett Packard LaserJet printer. Using a Hewlett Packard LaserJet driver with the printer set to the correct mode should provide good results. You may find that there is a sort of generic driver that matches a troublesome peripheral, although with this type of driver you may find that some of the more advanced facilities of the printer (or whatever) are not supported.

The peripherals that are most likely to cause problems are the Windows variety. A lot of internal modems and inexpensive printers fall into this category. The problem with devices of this type is that they lack most of the electronics that you would normally expect them to include. They are effectively incomplete devices that rely on the PC's hardware and a program to compensate for the missing hardware. As modern PCs have a substantial amount of "overkill" when used in many applications this system normally works very well, and enables peripheral devices to be produced at relatively low cost. The main drawback of this method is that it is difficult to use such peripherals with any other operating system. The driver software for a Windows device is clearly much more than a normal driver. It is probably possible to use any Windows device with another operating system such as Linux, but due to the complexity of the driver software a suitable driver may never be produced.

Preparation

Before you try to install Linux it will be necessary to do a certain amount of preparation. If you are starting with a new computer having a hard disc drive that is completely empty there is little to do. It is basically just a matter of trying to find some basic details of the hardware in case they are needed during installation. The same is true if you are going to install Linux on a computer that has previously been used with another operating system, but that operating system has been removed, together with any partitions on the hard disc. If you are installing Linux on a PC that has been used with another operating system, and all trace of the previous system has not been removed, the previous system must be removed before Linux can be installed. One way of doing this is to use the MS/DOS FDISK program, but there is probably nothing to be gained in doing things this way. The Linux version of FDISK is used to set up the required disc partitions during the installation process, and it can be used to remove the old partitions first. Note that Linux uses a different disc format to MS/DOS and any form of Windows, so any partitions left over from these can not be used as the basis of a Linux installation.

Dual boot

Matters are a little trickier if you have opted for a dual boot system where Linux will be used alongside another operating system such as Windows 98. Such an arrangement is perfectly possible, and I have used several dual boot systems of various types over a period of several years. A dual boot system requires a boot manager program, which basically hijacks the boot-up process and offers you a choice of operating systems. You simply select the one you require and the boot manager then boots-up that operating system, which should then work in the normal fashion. It does not matter if you do not have a boot manager program since Linux comes complete with one in the form of Lilo, the Linux loader program.

In order to produce a dual boot system you should first put the non-Linux operating system onto the computer. Linux will install alongside most other operating systems without too much trouble, but other operating systems are unlikely to be as tolerant of Linux. If you put Linux onto the computer and then install another operating system, Linux will probably remain intact on the hard disc, but the computer will almost certainly boot straight into the other operating system. Certainly expect this to happen if you add Windows 95 or 98 to a Linux system.

Matters become trickier still if you wish to add Linux to a computer that already has a well-tried and used system installed. Although it is unlikely that Linux will do any damage to an existing operating system unless you make a drastic mistake during installation, such mistakes are not difficult to make. It is as well to heed Sod's law in these situations. If something can go wrong it will! Do not try to add Linux onto an existing installation unless the existing system, or at least any important files it contains, can be reliably backed-up. It is unlikely that there will be any hard disc space that is totally unused (i.e. not partitioned and formatted), and you must therefore clear some space before installing Linux. It is important to leave sufficient spare capacity for the existing operating system to operate properly. Bear in mind that some programs, particularly graphics types, can require large amounts of hard disc space for temporary file storage. You must also leave sufficient space for any data files you may generate in the future or programs you will wish to load onto the disc. As pointed out previously, a worthwhile Linux installation will require a few hundred megabytes of hard disc space. In order to produce a dual boot system it will probably be necessary to have about one GB or more of spare disc capacity.

The long route to freeing up a section of hard disc for a Linux installation is to back up the existing system, and then repartition the disc using the MS/DOS FDISK program. Instead of partitioning the disc so that all its capacity is used, you leave sufficient unused capacity for the Linux installation. By repartitioning the disc the existing system is destroyed, and it has to be restored using the backup copy. The computer is then ready for Linux to be installed. The quick way to freeing up some hard disc space is to use a program such as PartitionMagic that enables the partitioning to be altered without destroying the existing operating system and the other files on the hard disc. Programs of this type do not guarantee to give perfect results every time, although in my experience they are pretty reliable. Anyway, it is still necessary to back up the existing system just in case it comes to grief during the repartitioning.

Before repartitioning the disc you need to make sure that the existing files are clumped together in a single lump and not liberally spread across the disc. Otherwise you might reclaim disc space that is occupied by files. Windows 95 and 98 have a built-in disc-defragmenting program. This is accessed via the menu system using Start, Programs, Accessories, System Tools, and Disk Defragmenter. Disc partitioning software often has this facility built-in, and may automatically defragment the disc before carrying out the repartitioning. Distributions of Linux are usually supplied with a simple disc-partitioning program such as Fips. This will usually perform any required repartitioning successfully, but requires the disc to be defragmented first.

Frankly, unless you are fairly expert at dealing with partitioning and installing operating systems it is probably best not to opt for a dual boot system. It is not actually that difficult, but for the inexperienced user it represents a golden opportunity to make a complete mess of the computer, and with the partitioning seriously messed up it can sometimes be difficult to retrieve the situation. Installing Linux onto a cheap second-hand or old and otherwise unused PC is a much easier and safer way of trying out this operating system.

Getting started

If you have bought a set of Linux discs complete with manuals it obviously makes sense to follow the instructions in the manual, which will give a detailed account of how to install that particular version of Linux. If you have a magazine disc version of Linux there will probably be little or no guidance to help with installation. As the exact method of installation varies from one distribution to another and from one version to the next, it is only possible to give some general guidance here. As you are installing what is essentially the same thing regardless of which distribution you are using, the general procedure is much the same. Many of the steps involved are perfectly straightforward, so we will concentrate here on the more awkward aspects of installation.

In order to install Linux you normally have to boot-up the computer into a sort of mini-Linux so that the installation software can be run. In the past it was sometimes necessary to produce a set of boot discs in order to get Linux installed, but boot discs are not normally required these days. If you buy a "boxed" version of Linux it may be supplied with a boot disc, but I would suggest that this is only used if other methods of booting prove to be problematic. Modern distributions of Linux are often supplied on a bootable CD-ROM and with this in the CD-ROM drive it is possible to boot from the CD-ROM straight into the basic version of Linux and the installation program. However, if you put the CD-ROM in the drive and then try to boot-up from it do not be surprised if the computer refuses to co-operate. For this method to work three criteria have to be met. First, the CD-ROM must be a bootable type. If it is, and these days most are, the literature supplied with the CD-ROM should say so. Next, the computer must support this boot-up method. Any new computer should support this feature, as do most that are no more than a few years old. It is not usually supported by PCs that are based on 80386, 80486, or early Pentium computers. Finally, a PC will only boot from a

CD-ROM if the correct boot options have been set in the BIOS Setup program.

If you wish to try booting from the CD-ROM it will almost certainly be necessary to go into the Setup program and select a suitable boot option. Also, if you are not sure whether or not your PC supports this boot method, the only sure way to find out is to look at the boot options available in the Setup program. It is only fair to point out here that inexpert use of the Setup program could prevent the computer from operating properly. The chances of doing any damage to the hardware are probably remote or non-existent, but if you scramble the settings it could be difficult to get everything set up correctly again. It is probably best not to try this method of booting up the computer unless you are reasonably experienced at dealing with PCs. Even if you are an experienced PC user, it is still essential to proceed with due care.

By far the most common way of entering the Setup program is to press the Delete key when the BIOS is going through its testing sequence, immediately after switching on the computer. At the appropriate time an on-screen message will appear. There are various other ways into the Setup program though, and if the Delete key method does not work you must consult the instruction manual for your PC. This should explain how to enter the Setup program and should give at least some brief details of the options available.

Once into the Setup program you must locate the section that deals with the boot-up options. The PC's manual or the manual for its motherboard may help here, or you may have to do some exploring. With a modern Award BIOS the initial screen (Figure 1.1) has a menu offering several further screens, and it is the "BIOS Features" screen that is required. When you enter this page (Figure 1.2) select the "Boot Sequence" section, and then cycle through the various options to see what is on offer. Choose any option that has CD-ROM as the first boot option. Then return to the main menu, select "Save And Exit Setup", and then press the "Y" key to actually save the changes and exit. Provided the CD-ROM drive and the Linux installation CD are co-operative, the PC should then boot into the mini-Linux operating system and the installation program. If it fails to do so, either the CD-ROM is not a bootable type, or the CD-ROM drive is not one that the BIOS can boot from. There is usually no problem when using an ordinary ATAPI CD-ROM drive, but drives using other interfaces are unlikely to be usable as the boot drive.

A modern AMI BIOS has a sort of simple graphical used interface, complete with support for some types of mouse. Select the "Advanced"

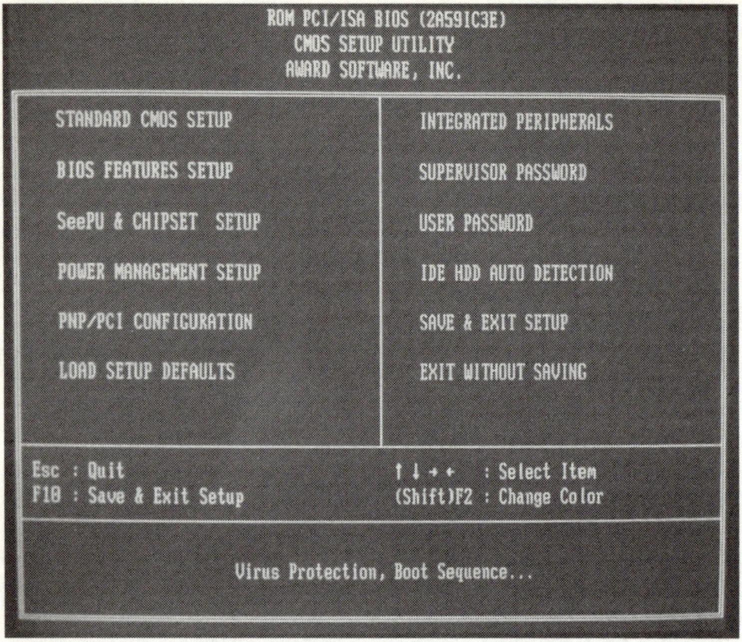

Fig.1.1 Select "BIOS FEATURES SETUP" from the main menu

option from the initial screen (Figure 1.3), and then "First Boot Device" from the next screen (Figure 1.4). Select "CD-ROM", and then return to the main menu. Click the mouse on the small box in the top left hand corner of the window to exit the main menu, and then click on the "Save Changes And Exit" box to actually save the new set-up information. It should then be possible to boot from the Linux installation CD. Note that once the Linux installation process has been completed you must return to the Setup program and restore the original boot settings. The computer may fail to boot correctly from the hard drive unless this is done.

Direct from CD-ROM

If you can not boot from the CD-ROM for one reason or another it should still be possible to install Linux direct from the CD-ROM. In order to do this you need to boot the computer into MS/DOS from a floppy disc, and CD-ROM support will also be needed. The easiest way to do this is to use a Windows 98 start-up disc, which is normally made during the Windows 98 installation process. A start-up disc can be made from a PC running Windows 98 by selecting Start, Settings, Control Panel, Add/Remove Programs, Startup Disk, and then operating the "Create Disk" button. A blank formatted 1.44-MB disc should be placed in drive A prior to operating the "Create Disk" button. With the disc in the drive at switch-on or after a system reset the computer will probably boot from the floppy disc. If not, you must go into the BIOS Setup program and set the floppy drive as the first boot drive. During the boot-up process a simple menu will appear, and the option of CD-ROM support should be selected.

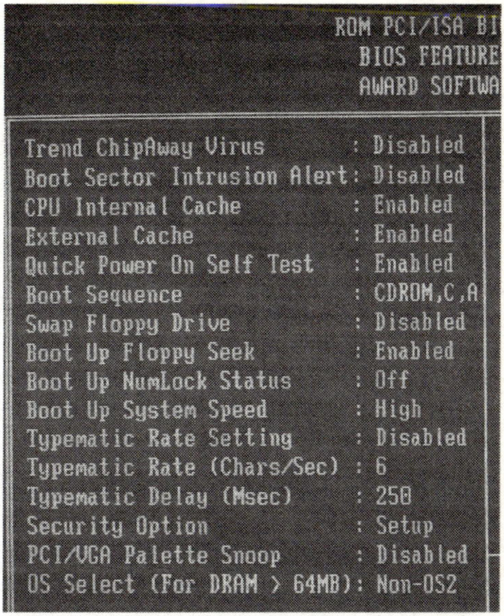

Fig.1.2 Select an option that has CDROM as the first boot device

Alternatively, a floppy disc can be formatted using MS/DOS. To make the disc bootable the /s option should be used when issuing the format command, as shown below:

format A: /s

It is also possible to add the system files to an ordinary formatted floppy disc using the SYS program supplied with MS/DOS. This is the instruction that would be used:

sys A:

Note that the Format and Sys commands are not internal parts of MS/DOS, and that the computer must be able to access the relevant program files for either of these to work.

Having made a boot-up disc it is then a matter of booting up the computer using the disc, and then adding CD-ROM support to the boot disc. The

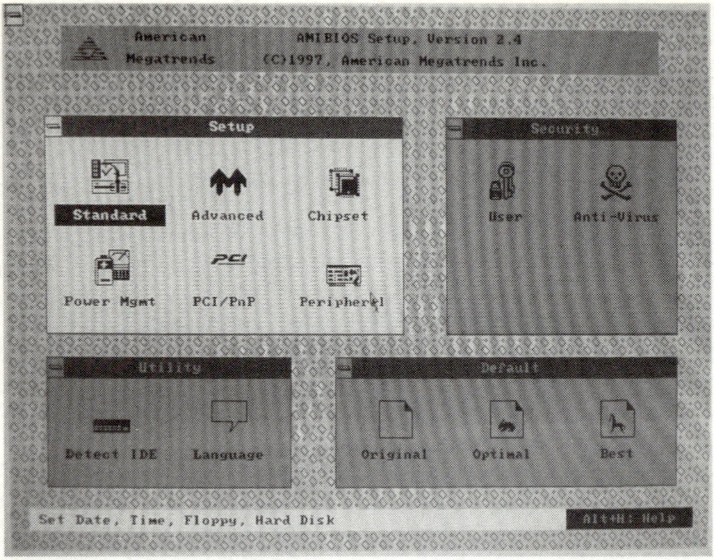

Fig.1.3 Select the "Advanced" menu

computer or CD-ROM drive should be supplied with the necessary installation software. It will then be necessary to reboot so that the added CD-ROM support takes effect, and you have access to the CD-ROM drive.

It is then a matter of exploring the files on the CD-ROM to track down the file that is used to launch the installation process. There may be a program file called something like setup.exe or install.exe, or perhaps a batch file called something like boot.bat or autoboot.bat. There will be some readme files on the CD, and one of these should tell you what you need to know. When you have located the appropriate file it is just a matter of running it to start the installation procedure. It is likely that the process will come to an abrupt halt if you launch the program from the root directory of the CD by specifying the path to the file. It is safer to go into the directory that contains the file and run it from there.

Questions and answers

Once into the installation process it is largely a matter of answering a series of questions. It may take a while to get to the first question, with numerous obscure messages appearing on the screen first. These

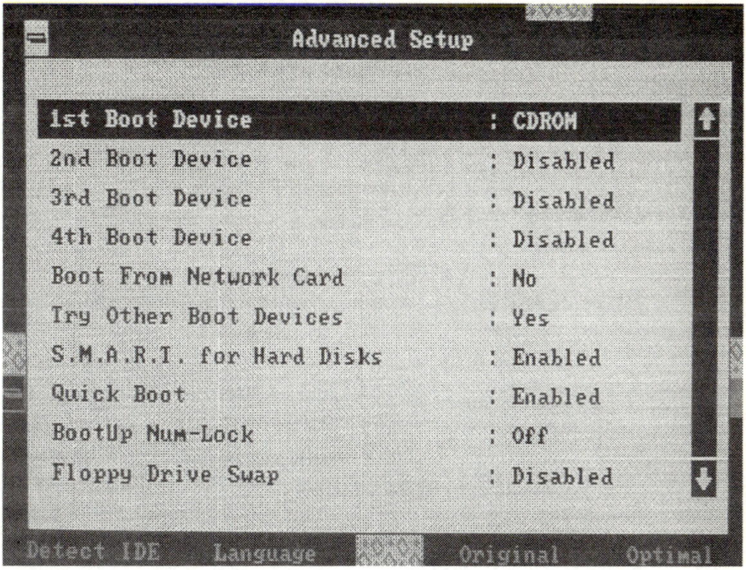

Fig.1.4 Set the first boot device as "CDROM"

messages tell you what the computer is doing as it boots into a sort of minimalist version of Linux, but unless you are a Linux expert most of the messages will not make a great deal of sense. Just ignore them and wait patiently for the installation program to run.

Many of the questions are very simple and just require you to select such things as the language to be used and the time zone you are in. Some Linux distributions are supplied with an installation program that will probe the computer to detect the hardware in use, and then install Linux with minimal input from the user. If this option is available, and it works with your particular PC, it is probably best to use it. Not all Linux installation programs are this obliging, and an automatic installation may not work with your particular PC anyway. It is then necessary to give the installation program some help. A common complaint about Linux installation programs is that they make it difficult to go back one step if you make a mistake. Be careful what keys you press or you may find yourself having to redo a complete section of the installation from scratch.

Disc partitioning

As explained previously, before starting the installation process some empty hard disc space is set aside for the Linux installation, but this hard disc space needs to be partitioned and formatted before Linux can utilize it. The partitioning is achieved using the Linux FDISK program, which is similar to the MS/DOS program of the same name. FDISK will be run early in the installation process, and you may be required to manually control the partitioning process. This is not too difficult, but you need to proceed carefully in order to avoid problems later on. If you are installing Linux alongside another operating system you need to be very careful indeed as mistakes could easily result in the other operating system being deleted.

Many PCs running Windows have the entire hard disc, even if it is a high capacity disc, set to operate as a single drive. This disc will usually be designated as drive C. Consequently, many Windows users are probably unfamiliar with the concept of hard disc partitioning. It is a very simple idea, whereby a single drive can be used as if it was actually two or more smaller drives. Rather than using a 6.4 GB drive as a single drive it could be used as two 3.2 GB drives. These would be designated as drives C and D. The extra partition or partitions are notional drives and not separate pieces of hardware, and they are called logical drives. There can be advantages in splitting a drive into smaller parts, especially where a PC is fitted with a very large drive. There can be drawbacks as well, not the least of which is that you can end up with several small sections of unused disc space which are not very useful. One large chunk of disc space of identical total capacity would generally be more useful.

With Linux there are usually a minimum of two partitions on the disc. As explained previously, some of the disc is normally assigned to the swap disc, which is disc capacity that is used for temporary storage by the operating system. Windows can have a permanent swap disc of this type, and it can bring performance advantages. However, most Windows installations just use any spare capacity on the main disc for temporary file storage. The swap disc partition is normally at least equal to the amount of RAM fitted to the PC, and it can be made larger than this if there is sufficient hard disc capacity. The maximum size for this partition is 100 MB. If your PC has 32 MB or memory, you would therefore have a swap disc size of at least 32 MB, but could go as far as 100 MB if there is plenty of spare hard disc capacity. With a PC having 128 MB of memory the swap disc would have to be the maximum of 100 MB, or as close to this as the available disc space permitted. The rest of the available disc capacity could be split into further partitions, but there is probably no point in doing so. Particularly if the amount of disc space available is not very large, it is advisable to use one partition for the main Linux installation.

Using FDISK

The FDISK program uses a simple command line interface, where you issue commands by typing in the appropriate letter and then pressing the Return key. Any numeric data required by the program is also typed in at the command line. This is a list of the commands available when using FDISK:

Letter	Command
a	Toggle a bootable flag on current partition
d	Delete current partition
l	List all partitions
m	Main menu
n	Create a new partition
p	Print a list of partitions with partition details
q	Quit without saving changes
r	Replace the system ID of the current partition
u	Modify the display/entry units (cylinders or sectors)
v	Verify
w	Save changes and exit

For the sake of this example we will assume that the PC is to be used solely with Linux, and that it has a hard disc capacity of 1000 MB. With (say) 32 MB of memory you will require a swap disc of at least 32 MB, but might decide that a slightly larger capacity of 50 MB would be better. This represents about five percent of the total disc space, which means that 95 percent is to be used for the main Linux installation. Create the main partition first, and pressing the "N" key (followed by the Return key of course). The computer responds with:

Command action

e Extended

p Primary partition (1-4)

You are being asked to select the partition type, and it is a primary partition that is required. Press the "P" key followed by Return. The computer responds with:

Partition number (1 - 4)

The partition being created is the first one on the hard disc, so type "1" followed by Return. You will then be asked to specify the numbers for the start and finish cylinders for the new partition, and the program will display the range of available numbers. As the hard disc is not being used with any other operating systems the first available cylinder should be number one. The highest number available depends on the size and characteristics of the disc, but for this example we will assume that there are 800 cylinders available. We wish to use the first 95 percent of the available cylinders, which works out at cylinders from 1 to 760. As an alternative to specifying the last cylinder you can enter the size of the partition in megabytes or kilobytes. For instance, typing "+950M" followed by Return would set the partition at 950 MB. This second method is perhaps easier than specifying the final cylinder number, but you need to be careful, as there is something less than complete agreement about what constitutes a megabyte. It is easy to end up with an amount of space for the swap disc that is somewhat larger or smaller than you intended.

Next the partition for the swap disc must be created, and this is basically just a matter or repeating the steps above. This is the second partition on the disc, so give "2" as the partition number. The program should indicate the first and last cylinder numbers for the unused disc space. As we wish to use all this space for the swap disc, these numbers are used when setting the size of this partition. In our example installation the start and finish numbers will be 761 and 800. This creates the partition for the swap disc, but at present it is a standard Linux partition. It must be changed to a swap partition before it can be used for the swap disc. To do this press "T" followed by Return, and then "2" followed by a further Return to select the correct partition. The computer will respond with:

Hex code (type L to list codes):

If you type "L" followed by return you will be greeted with quite a large list of available partition types. At present the partition is type 83 (native Linux), and it must be changed to type 82 (Linux swap). To do this simply type "82" followed by Return. It is as well to check at this stage to see if everything has been set up correctly. Type "P" and then Return to bring up the partition table. In our example this would bring up something like:

Device	Boot	Start	End	Blocks	Id	System
/tmp/hda1		1	760	781234	83	Linux native
/tmp/hda2		761	800	39062	82	Linux swap

The entries under "Device" are the equivalents of MS/DOS and Windows drive letters. This is something that is handled rather differently in Linux, and this subject is covered in detail in the next chapter. The important things to check are the sizes of the two partitions and that they are the correct types. If the partition types have been accidentally swapped over, they can be corrected using partition type command. If an error in the sizes has been made you will have to delete both partitions and start again. To delete a partition type "D" followed by Return, and then type the number of the partition to be deleted followed by a further Return.

Unlike the MS/DOS version of FDISK, the Linux version will not automatically make the first primary partition bootable. This is a common cause of problems when installing Linux as the sole operating system on a computer. If you omit this step the installation will proceed more or less normally, and everything will probably seem to be perfectly all right. At least, it will until you next use the computer. The computer then starts the boot-up process but simply hangs up or goes into a loop printing garbage down the screen. To make the first primary partition bootable press the "A" key followed by Return. The computer will respond with:

Partition number (1 - 4)

It is the first primary partition that must be made bootable, so press the "1" key followed by Return. To check that this has worked correctly print the partition table on the screen again. If all is well it should look something like this:

Device	Boot	Start	End	Blocks	Id	System
/tmp/hda1	*	1	760	781234	83	Linux native
/tmp/hda2		761	800	39062	82	Linux swap

To actually write the new partition information onto the hard disc press "W" followed by Return. You are then ready to continue with the installation process. If the installation program asks you if there are any more changes to be made to the partitioning, answer no and continue with the installation. You may be asked to specify the mount point of the disc file system. Simply give this as "/". Note that when dealing with MS/DOS and Windows file names it is the backslash (\) character that is used to indicate a jump from one directory to another. With Linux the forward slash (/) character is used in much the same way. If you are a hardened MS/DOS or Windows user it may take some time to adjust to the change, and you will have to put up with a lot of error messages in the meantime!

Next you will be asked what partition you wish to use as the swap disc. As there is only one partition of the correct type the computer should offer the correct one as the default. This partition with then be formatted. A similar process is then used to select the partition to be used for the installation. Again, with only one partition of the correct type the correct partition should be offered as the default option. When selecting both partitions there will be the option of checking for errors, or "verifying" the disc as it might be called. If you are using an old computer it might be worthwhile checking the hard disc for errors. Otherwise it is probably not worthwhile, and with a large hard disc the verification process can take a long time.

Software selection

With most installation programs you will be given at least some control over the packages to be installed. There can be a choice of various standard installations along the lines of small, medium, large, and very large, and you will probably have the choice of selecting individual packages or groups of programs of various types. This is obviously a personal choice to some extent, but it is advisable to start with a fairly complete installation if your hard disc will accommodate it. This leaves your options open and enables you to experiment to the full with Linux. In order to get the most from Linux you will need the X Windows system and some of the X Windows applications. Software such as the C and C++ development tools is likely to be of little interest to most users.

There will inevitably be some questions pertaining to networking. Here we are only concerned with Linux used on a workstation, but you can not totally ignore its networking capability. In effect you have to install Linux as part of a network, but not actually networked to anything. Obviously you just answer no if the installation program asks if a network card is installed in the computer. At some stage a host name will probably be requested, and the name will be required even though there is no network. Either accept the default name, which will be something like "nodomain.nowhere", or replace it with a name of your own choice. The basic format of the name must be the same as the default name.

LILO

Linux normally boots-up via a program called LILO, and this may need a certain amount of configuration prior to installation. Unless you know what you are doing is it basically just a matter of selecting the default options. If it is necessary to select the place in which LILO will be installed, choose the master boot record (MBR) of the first primary partition of the hard disc. LILO can provide a delay before it boots Linux, but this facility is mainly included for dual boot systems where the delay enables the user to select an alternative operating system if desired. With a PC that is used solely for Linux you may like to reduce the delay if this option is offered.

You may also be asked to select the Linux kernel to install. Unless you know exactly what you are doing and have good reason to do so, simply opt for the default kernel.

Passwords

During the installation process you will be asked to provide at least one password. As a minimum, the password for the supervisor or root account must be provided. By logging in as the system supervisor (also known as the superuser) you have full access to the system and can alter any system settings, install and delete programs, etc. You may also be required to set up at least one user account. Even where there will only be one user, many prefer not to log in as the supervisor for everyday use of the computer. By signing in as an ordinary user you eliminate the risk of accidentally making unwanted changes to the system. As an ordinary user you are more or less limited to running programs and using your own data files. A user account or accounts can be produced later if only the root account is set up during the installation process. If you are asked for a group ID during this section of the installation process, simply accept the defaults.

The installation program will give some guidance about choosing an acceptable password, but it normally has to be five or more characters in length, and can consist of upper and lower case letters, plus numbers and punctuation marks. The more random the password the harder it will be for anyone to hack their way into the system, but the harder it will be for the user to remember. If you should forget the root password it will not be possible to make changes to the Linux installation, and it might become necessary to reinstall Linux. Do not use the popular and predictable passwords such as the date of your birthday or your name spelled backwards. Better choices are random words with a deliberate misspelling (e.g. bellweing rather than wellbeing) or the place where your mother was born but spelled backwards. These should stick in your mind but should not be easy for anyone to crack.

X Windows

Assuming you have elected to install the X Windows system, this will probably require a certain amount of manual configuration. With some recent versions of Linux the installation process will try to determine the hardware present by a system of software probing. If this is successful you will not have to do any manual configuration, but it is likely that the probing process will be less than completely successful. You will then have to provide some information about the type of mouse in use, the amount of memory on the video card, or something of this nature.

Manual configuration is normally achieved using the XF86Setup program. If asked if you wish to run this now or later I would suggest you select the "Now" option, but this will bring up a message screen explaining that "Now" actually means it will be postponed until a little later! When the configuration program is finally run it provides an initial help screen (Figure 1.5), which helps with navigation around the program. Some information about the type of mouse in use is usually requested prior to the XF86Setup program being run, and with luck the mouse will be working from the outset. It is then very easy to navigate your way around the program. If not, the first page of XF86Setup is the one that configures the mouse (Figure 1.6), and the keyboard must be used to control this until the mouse is working. Assuming you know exactly what type of mouse you are using there should be no problem getting it to work properly.

One area of confusion concerns Logitech mice. The Logitech mouse option does not work with modern Logitech serial mice, and does not even work with my slightly ancient Logitech mouse. Unless you have a "genuine antique" Logitech mouse it is the Microsoft option that should be used. If there is a generic serial mouse option this should also work with practically any serial mouse. Many computers are supplied with serial mice that are not produced by one of the main mice manufacturers. Again, the Microsoft or generic serial mouse options should give good

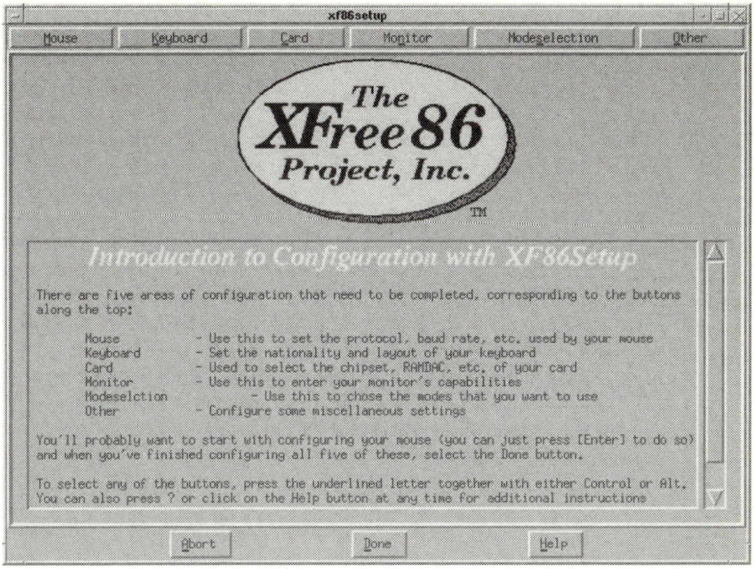

Fig.1.5 The initial XF86 help screen

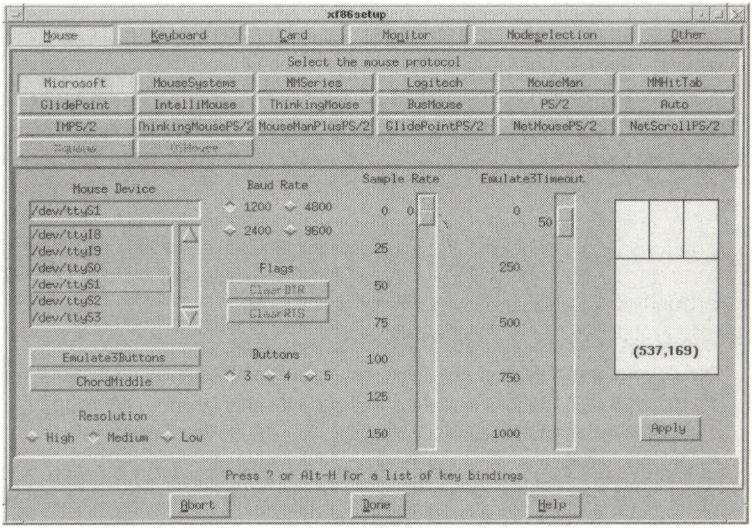

Fig.1.6 The mouse configuration page

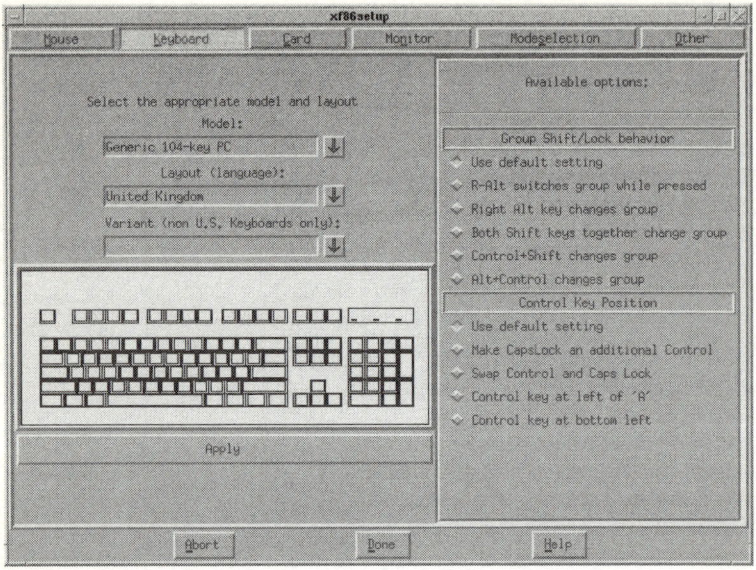

Fig.1.7 The keyboard setup page should need little attention

results. Virtually all serial mice will work using the Microsoft or generic serial mouse driver. For a serial mouse to work properly X Windows must be set to use the correct mouse port. If you are using a bus or mouse port mouse there should be no problem, and the configuration program should default to the correct port. Most PCs have two serial ports, and you may have to manually select the correct one. This is the normal correlation between Linux and MS/DOS or Windows port identifications.

MS/DOS	**Linux**
Port 1 (COM1)	/dev/tty0
Port 2 (COM2)	/dev/tty1

The names used for the ports are not fully standardised, and the serial ports could be called something like /dev/cua0 and /dev/cua1. If necessary experiment a little to find the right port setting.

There are some options such as mouse sensitivity that can be set to suit individual preferences. Other options such as the baud rate should not be altered unless there is good reason to do so. As explained previously, in theory Linux requires a three-button mouse, but you can use a two-

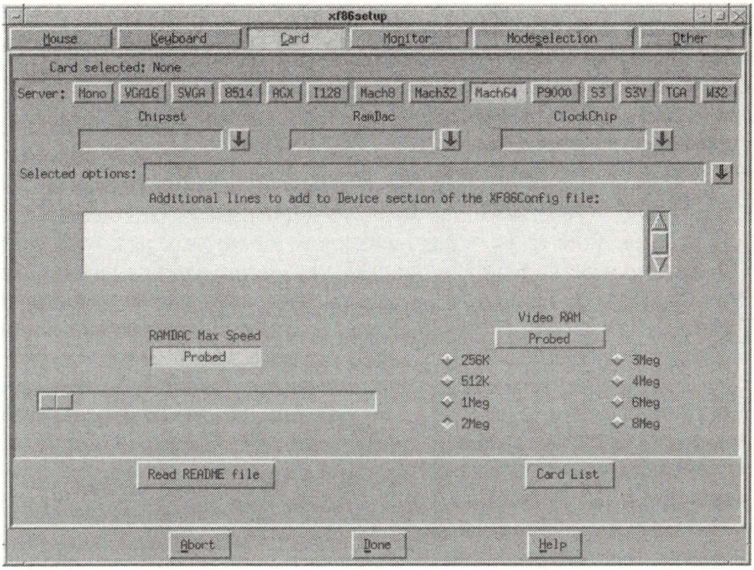

Fig.1.8 The screen that deals with the video card settings

button mouse plus a three-button emulation mode. In practice the third button seems to be of little importance these days, but if you are using a two-button mouse it might be as well to activate the three-button emulation.

Keyboard

The next screen of the configuration program is for the keyboard (Figure 1.7). The keyboard should be working reasonably well already, and it is not normally essential to alter any settings. If the language setting is wrong it clearly makes sense to correct it, but it is probably best to leave everything else unaltered. You can always return to the configuration later if some aspect of keyboard operation is incorrect or you wish to "fine tune" the key functions.

Video card

For X Windows to work with your video card it must have a suitable server. A server is roughly equivalent to a driver program in Windows terminology. With Windows the video driver might be one supplied as part of Windows, but it is often a program provided by the video card manufacturer. Linux support from hardware manufacturers is still a bit "thin on the ground", and the X server will normally be one of those provided with Linux. You may have to select the required servers early in the installation process, or they may all have been installed. If the required servers have to be selected I would suggest that the standard VGA server is included in your selection. This will only operate at 640 by 480 pixel resolution with 16 colours, but it should work with any normal video card. For operation at higher resolution with more colours it is necessary to use a server that has support for the particular video card in use. I would suggest that any likely looking servers be installed so that your options are left open. If necessary, you can then experiment with various servers in an attempt to find one that works properly. If a SVGA server is available it might be worthwhile installing this as well. The SVGA offers operation at higher resolution than the VGA type, and is worth trying if you can not find specific support for your video card. It is unlikely to utilize the full capabilities of the video card though.

The video configuration page (Figure 1.8) enables various parameters to be set by the user, but provided you have selected a suitable server it should not be necessary to do so. The program can use probing of the card to find out what it needs to know. It is only necessary to set things manually if the probing fails for some reason. Apparently the probing can sometimes cause a malfunction, and could result in the computer hanging up, but I have not experienced such problems except when an unsuitable server had been selected. If a list of compatible cards for the server is provided, and if your video card is included in the list it clearly makes sense to select this option. This will virtually guarantee correct operation of the video card with X Windows.

Monitor

The next screen covers monitor selection (Figure 1.9). It is unlikely that your monitor will be included in the list of models supported, although some recent Linux distributions do have a large number to choose from. If there is no specific support for your monitor it does not really matter. By selecting the parameters manually virtually any monitor can be accommodated. The instruction manual for the monitor should provide the necessary facts and figures. In order to get the most from X Windows software a fairly high resolution is required, and I recommend a minimum of 1024 x 768 if your monitor supports high resolutions. On the other hand, high resolution can be difficult to use if the monitor is small or it only supports low frame rates. A frame rate of 70 hertz or more is needed to give a genuinely flicker-free picture that is easy on the eye when used for long periods. At least a good 15-inch monitor is needed for operation

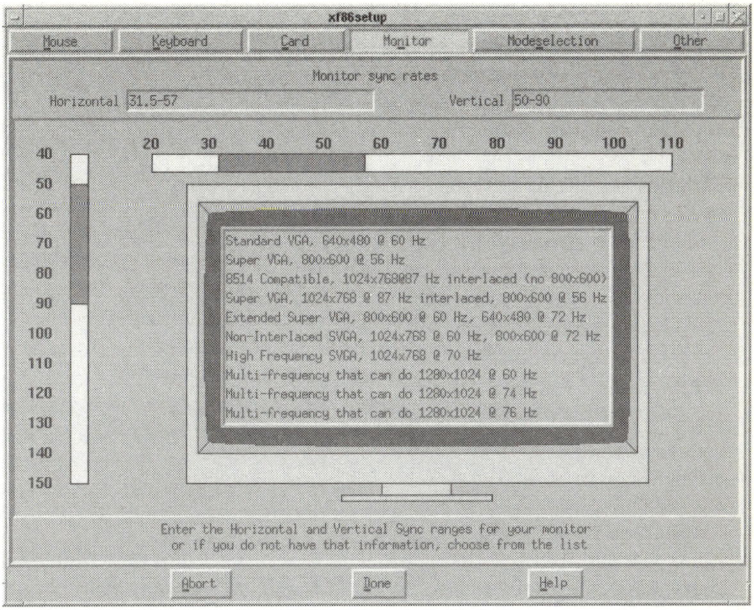

Fig.1.9 The monitor setup screen is used to set scan frequencies, etc.

at 1024 by 768 without eyestrain. It is probably better to settle for 800 by 600 pixel operation if the size of the screen is less than 15 inches or the monitor does not support high scan rates at high resolutions.

In the initial setting up you are telling the X server the capabilities of the monitor, but you are not actually selecting the screen resolution that will be used. To do this you must-click on the "Mode Selection" tab at the top of the monitor configuration screen. This brings up a new screen (Figure 1.10) that makes it easy to select the desired screen resolutions. By default X Windows uses the highest resolution selected, and this resolution can be beyond the maximum resolution of the monitor. The monitor then displays as much of the larger virtual screen as it can, and where necessary the view automatically scrolls when the cursor is placed near the edge of the screen. This type of thing tends to be rather confusing in use, and my preference is to keep the screen resolution no higher than the true resolution of the monitor.

The buttons near the bottom of the screen enable the colour depth (ie the number of colours available) to be chosen. The colour depth is chosen in terms of the number of bits used per pixel. This table shows

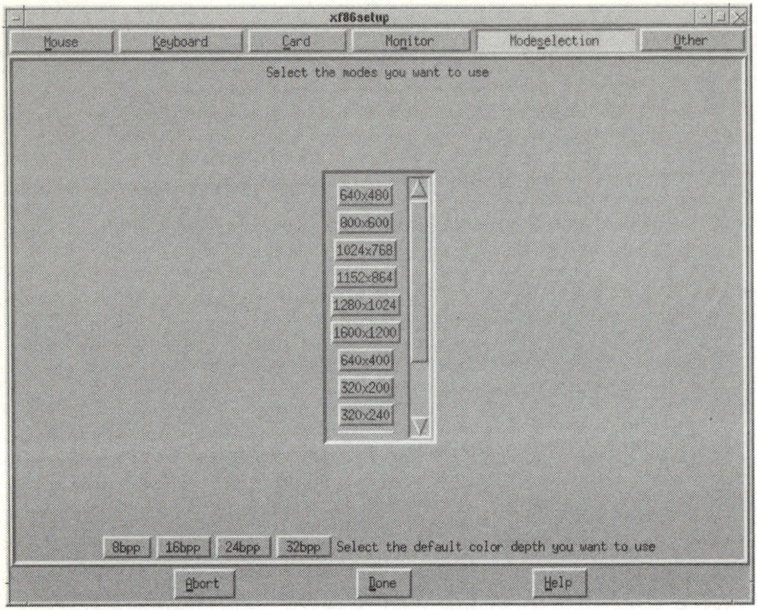

Fig.1.10 The screen used to select the required screen modes

the correlation between bits per pixel (bpp) and the actual number of colours available.

Bits per pixel	**Colours**
8	256
16	65536
24	16776950
32	Approx. 4.3 billion

The maximum number of colours available for a given (true) screen resolution depends on the amount of RAM fitted to the video card. Unless your computer is rather slow it makes sense to choose a fairly high colour depth, but for most purposes there is no point in going beyond 24-bit operation.

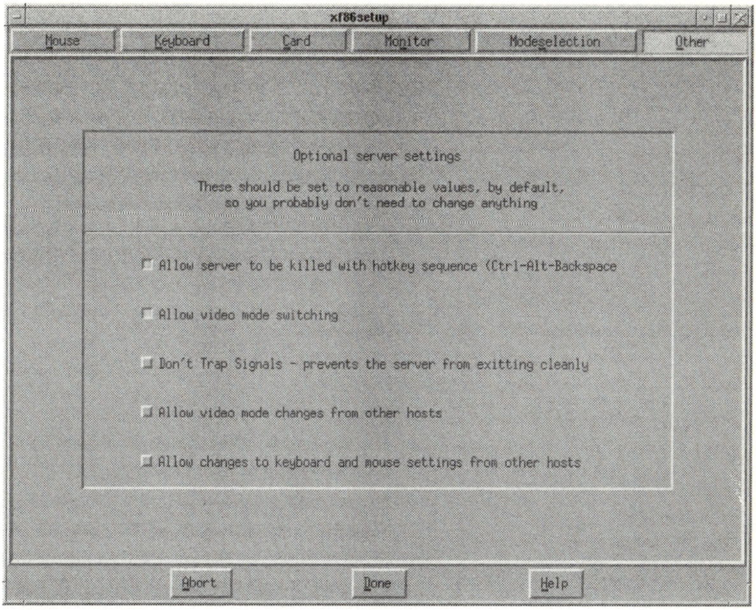

Fig.1.11 The "Other" screen configures minor functions

Other

The final tab at the top of the main configuration page brings up a screen (Figure 1.11) that enables miscellaneous factors to be controlled. These are concerned with switching screen resolutions on the fly, and with exiting X Windows. At this stage it is probably best to simply accept the default settings. Some of the options are irrelevant unless the computer is part of a network. By default the system will be set to use Control-Alt-Backspace as a means of exiting the X server. This is a useful facility as it permits an easy way back to normal Linux operation if you are greeted with a blank or scrambled screen on entering X Windows.

When everything has been set up to your satisfaction operate the "Done" tab to exit the XF86Config program. The program will then adjust everything to suit your video card and monitor settings, after which it will try to run the X server. If all is well you can exit the configuration program completely. You must rerun the XF86Config program if there is a major problem and the screen is far from correct. Minor problems with the display, such as too little width or height, can usually be corrected using the monitor's controls. If this fails to give satisfactory results you can use the Xvidtune program to make fine adjustments to the scan rates and other aspects of the video timing. I suppose that using Xvidtune is very slightly risky, so it is best to only use it if you really need to.

Testing, testing

Eventually you should end up with everything installed and Linux under way. Before you can use Linux it is necessary to log-in, and this requires a user name and the corresponding password. If you set up a user account during the installation process enter the appropriate name and press Return. Then when prompted for the password, enter the appropriate string of characters and press Return. You should then be into Linux and ready to start using the new operating system. If you did not set up a user account during installation it is still possible to go into Linux. You must log in as the system supervisor. For the user name enter "root" and then press Return. Then type in the password and press Return again. Linux will then be up and running, awaiting your first commands.

At this point it is a good idea to close down Linux, switch off the computer, and then switch on again to check that Linux will boot properly from a "cold" start. If it fails to do so, go through the installation process again, making sure that the appropriate disc partition is bootable, etc. It is not a good idea to shut down Linux by simply switching off the computer. As with Windows 95 and 98, this leaves various temporary files on the hard disc drive, and things left somewhat "up in the air". The correct way to close down Linux is to use the shutdown command, and to only switch off the computer once the string of on-screen messages finish. The final message should say something like "system halted".

The shutdown command has various switches and controls that can be used to govern the exact way in which it functions. Bear in mind here that Linux is designed for use with a network that will probably be switched off infrequently, and could have many users. The shutdown command would normally be issued together with a shutdown time, and a message warning of the shutdown time would then be sent to each terminal. All this is of no consequence if Linux is used on a workstation, and you simply want to close down the system immediately at the end of each session. For an immediate shutdown use this command;

shutdown -h now

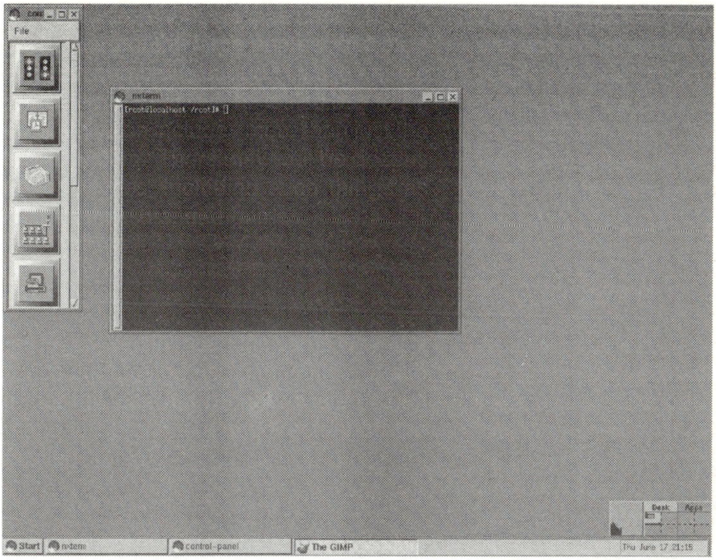

Fig.1.12 The opening X Windows screen in Red Hat Linux 5.2

Linux is usually case sensitive, and the command examples given in this book will only work if they are copied precisely. In most cases everything has to be in lower case letters, but there are some exceptions.

Having rebooted the system successfully the next step is to check that X Windows is functioning correctly. By default Linux does not usually run X Windows automatically at start-up, but some systems do now do so. To start X Windows use this command:

startx

After a few seconds of frantic hard disc activity a graphical user interface should appear on the screen, but the exact appearance will depend on the distribution and version of Linux in use. Figure 1.12 and 1.13 respectively show the screens obtained from Red Hat Linux 5.2 and Caldera Open Linux 1.3. It is worthwhile experimenting with the menu systems and the mouse to get acquainted with the general way in which things function. However, if an alternative desktop environment such as KDE was included in the installation, I would suggest exiting X Windows before too long and trying the alternative graphical front-end. If KDE or an alternative such as Gnome is available during installation I would strongly recommend including it in the installation. Most Linux

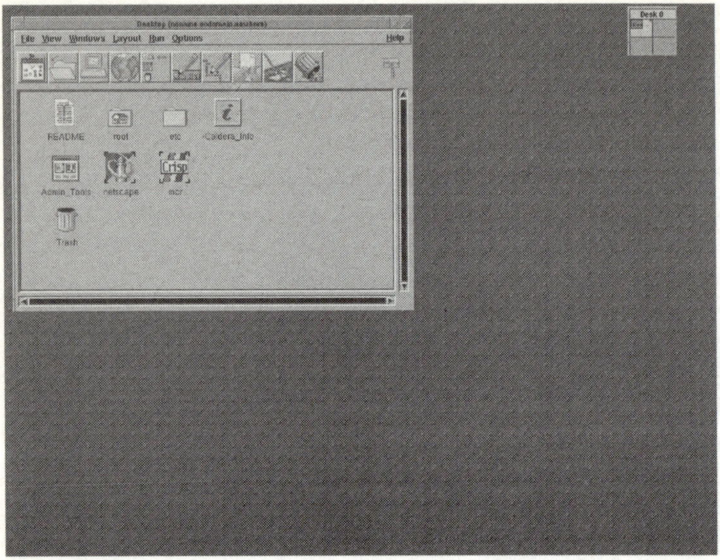

Fig.1.13 The opening X Windows screen in Caldera Open Linux 1.3

distributions now include KDE, and to follow much of the material in this book you must have KDE installed. Note that with some systems the "startx" command will actually run KDE. Once back at the Linux command prompt and assuming KDE is installed, it can be run using this command:

kde

When KDE has loaded the screen should look something like Figure 1.14, but the exact appearance depends on the version in use and the default settings. Using KDE is covered in chapters 3 and 4, and it will not be considered further here. However, by exploring the menu system you should have no difficulty in running a few programs such as some of the games.

Dual booting

As pointed out previously, Linux can be used in dual boot systems where you have the choice of booting into Linux or another operating system such as Windows 98. The installation process is similar with the dual boot approach, but at the hard disc partitioning stage there will already

Fig.1.14 The opening screen in KDE 1.0

be one or more partitions on the disc, which are the ones used by the existing operating system. The "p" option of Fdisk can be used to show the existing partitions before you start to allocate the free space to the Linux partitions. These partitions are produced using the same basic procedure that is used for a normal Linux installation, but the partition numbers will be higher due to the existing partitions. If there are already two primary partitions on the disc, the main Linux and Linux swap partitions would be partitions three and four. Remember that no more than four primary partitions can be accommodated. One partition will already be the bootable partition, and this will normally be left as the boot partition.

There is not usually any major problem in getting a PC to dual boot, but if it insists on booting straight into one or other of the operating systems it is worthwhile considering the floppy disc solution. This works on the basis of having Lilo installed onto a floppy disc rather than the hard disc. With this disc not in the drive at boot-up the computer will boot into the other operating system in the normal fashion. If the disc is in the drive, Lilo runs and boots Linux. It may appear as though Linux is booting from the floppy disc, but strictly speaking it is booting from the hard disc. Lilo points the boot-up process in the right direction, and from

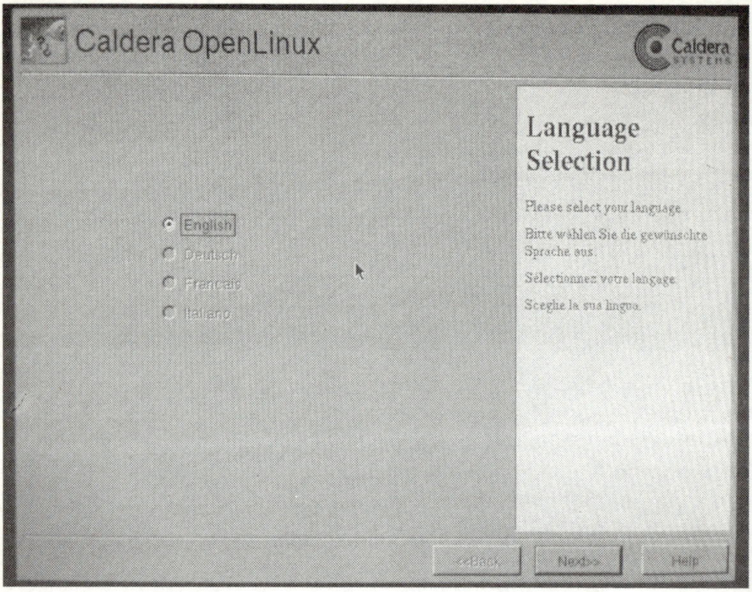

Fig.1.15 Caldera Open Linux 2.2 use a GUI during installation

there it boots-up Linux from the hard disc. This is a slightly crude way of doing things, but it is often very effective with computers that are otherwise reluctant to co-operate with dual booting.

If you wish to use a dual boot system but have little or no experience at dealing with operating systems it would probably be worthwhile obtaining a version of Linux that gives plenty of assistance with dual boot installation. Open Linux 2.2 for example, is supplied complete with special versions of the PartitionMagic and BootMagic programs. The program CD-ROM will run under Windows 95/98/NT, and enables the necessary hard disc space for Linux to be cleared. An installation Wizard then helps to get Linux installed correctly, and the text screen of most Linux installation programs is replaced by a graphical user interface. This has a "BACK" button which makes it easy to move back one or two stages to correct an error (Figures 1.15 and 1.16). It is not quite a case of putting the CD-ROM in the drive and then sitting back while the computer gets on with it, but these days installing Linux does not have to be any more difficult than installing Windows.

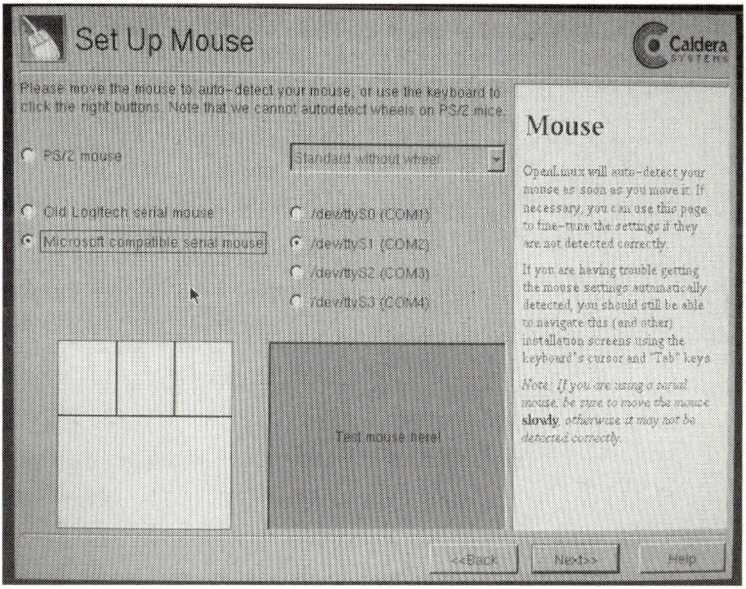

Fig.1.16 The Caldera Open Linux 2.2 mouse set-up screen

2

Command Line

What is it?

Anyone familiar with the early days of computing with PCs will have used the MS/DOS operating system, and will be familiar with the concept of the command line interpreter. Those who started with Windows 95, 98, or NT will probably be less familiar with this method of working. Modern versions of Windows still have a command line interpreter, and with Windows 95/98 there are two ways of utilizing it. You can either reboot the computer in MS/DOS mode, or you can run an MS/DOS window from within Windows. Even though there can be advantages in using a command line interpreter, most Windows users try to avoid doing so as much as possible. In fact it is likely that a fair percentage of Windows users have never used MS/DOS mode or an MS/DOS window. Linux now has graphical user interfaces and it is possible to largely avoid using the command line interpreter. Whether or not it is possible to do without it altogether depends on the features offered by the graphical user interface, and the types of task you will need to undertake. In most cases it is probably not yet possible to pretend the command line interpreter does not exist, unless you are prepared to accept some limitations on the way in which the system is used.

Even if you are not intending to make much use of the command line interpreter it is still advisable to look though this chapter. You may find some useful facilities here that can get you out of difficulties at some later date. Also, some of the material covered in this chapter is of a general nature, and is the type of thing that you will need to know even if you normally use a Windows style front-end to handle things like file manipulation. For example, this chapter covers the Linux directory structure, which is significantly different to that of Windows.

So what exactly is a command line interpreter? When Linux is booted up you are greeted with an on-screen message called a prompt, which should be something like this:

Login:

It will probably be headed by a Linux version number, a copyright notice, or something of this nature, but the important bit is the prompt which is telling you it is time to enter a name and start the login process. You respond by typing in the appropriate name and pressing the Return key. The computer then responds by asking for the password, or prints an error message and repeats the login prompt if you make a major mistake. At its most simple level this is all there is to using a command line interpreter. You type in commands or information requested by the computer, and it responds by carrying out the appropriate actions or printing an error message if there is something wrong with your input.

Computers are very unforgiving, and an error message will result if the information you type in contains even the smallest of errors. With short commands this is no great hardship, but with long and complex commands it can get rather tedious if it takes two or three attempts to get it right. It is partially this uncompromising approach that has made command line interpreters relatively unpopular. Another major factor is undoubtedly that graphical user interfaces look less intimidating and are more fun to use. No one is ever going to accuse command line interpreters of being user-friendly. On the other hand, typing in a command can almost instantly perform complex tasks that would be difficult or impossible using a graphical user interface.

With most Linux systems the computer is ready for command line input once it has booted up and a user has logged in. If your system automatically enters X Windows or KDE once the login has been completed you must exit the windowing program before commands can be entered. Alternatively, it should be possible to run a command line interpreter from within the windowing program. This is roughly analogous to running an MS/DOS window from within Windows 95 or 98. Whichever method you use, the results should be exactly the same.

Shells

When dealing with Linux you will often encounter the word "shell". This word is not totally unknown in the world of MS/DOS and Windows, but is little used. It is the means by which the operating system is controlled, and the command line interpreter is a shell. It can also mean a program that makes the basic command line interpreter easier to use, but does not go as far as a full graphical user interface. With MS/DOS the command line interpreter is not normally considered to be a shell, but is accepted as an integral part of the operating system. With Linux the situation is different, and the command line interpreter is effectively a normal Linux program that acts as an interface between the user and the Linux kernel. Linux has been produced in a layered fashion with various facilities being added around the basic shell. Software of this type is sometimes called "onion" software. MS/DOS utilizes a different arrangement with the internal commands built into the main program, and the lesser user external commands provided by separate add-on programs.

This is all largely irrelevant to the user, but you need to know that there is more than one shell available for Linux. In fact there are numerous Linux shells to choose from. This situation has arisen simply because some users felt that the original shell called *Bourne* was inadequate in some respects, so they produced their own "improved" version. Some of the improved shells were then improved further. This ability to add to and modify Linux is one of its big selling points. However, it is only of real use if you have the necessary expertise, can afford to pay someone to do the work for you, or can persuade a Linux guru that it would be an interesting project to undertake. During the Linux installation process you may be asked which shell you wish to use. Unless you have a good reason to choose a different one it is best to settle for the default option, which will almost certainly the shell called *bash*. This name is an in-joke, and is a contraction of *Bourne again shell*.

The examples in this chapter assume that *bash* is "up and running", so you need to be using *bash* or a fully compatible shell. If your Linux system boots straight into KDE or another desktop environment you can run these examples on a console from within the desktop, but it is probably better to exit the desktop and run them using the raw Linux shell. If you are not sure which shell is in use, try using this command:

echo $SHELL

This should produce a result something like:

/bin/bash

If you get no answer from this or an error message you have probably used lower case letters instead of upper case, or vice versa. This is a common cause of problems when those experienced with MS/DOS use a Linux system. MS/DOS is not case sensitive for filenames, commands, or anything at all. With Linux just about everything is case-sensitive, and to avoid endless error messages you should assume that absolutely everything is case sensitive. You must be careful to do things not just "to the letter", but "to the case" as well. If you get it right, this command will return the contents of the variable called "SHELL", which contains the name of the file that is providing the shell. It provides the name of the file and the subdirectory (folder) in which it is located. This should produce a result something like this:

/bin/bash

As pointed out previously, Linux uses the forward slash character rather than a backslash one to indicate changes from one subdirectory to another. The backslash character is used to continue a command onto another line incidentally. The answer returned by this command tells you that the file providing the shell is called "bash", and it is in the subdirectory called "bin". If the shell you are running is not *bash*, typing this command should run the *bash* shell:

bash

Again, make sure that you use letters of the correct case when typing this command. Once into the shell the command line prompt you see will depend on whether you have logged in as the supervisor (i.e. logged in as "root") or as a normal user. It also depends on the name of the system. On one of my systems the following is obtained when I login as "root":

[root@robert /root]#

Logging in as an ordinary user called (say) fred would give the following prompt:

[fred@robert /fred]$

In addition to the change in name, note that the hash (#) sign has changed to a dollars ($) character. The hash sign is displayed only for the system supervisor, and indicates that the user can make changes to system settings. It is effectively a warning that you have to be careful what you do, as you have access to files that govern the way the system operates. Careless use of these files could prevent the system from operating properly.

The first part of the prompt is simply the name of the user and the system. The second section indicates the current position in the file system. MS/DOS can be set up in a similar fashion, and if the system were currently in the subdirectory called "DOS" on drive C the prompt would look something like this:

C:/DOS>

Roots

For someone who has been using Windows and MS/DOS for years the Linux file system can take a little getting used to. In Windows and MS/DOS things tend to be rather more compartmentalised, with each disc drive having what is effectively its own discrete directory structure. You can go into a particular drive and examine its directories, but any directories on another disc can only be examined by changing over to that drive. With MS/DOS you can copy a file from a disc drive to a port, but the ports are again separate entities and not part of the file structure. With the recent versions of Windows the Windows Explorer program ties things together to a degree, with "My Computer" representing the overall system, and the disc drives, etc., sprouting out from this. The "My Computer" icon on the Windows desktop is also an attempt to unify the separate parts of the file system.

With Linux the file structure is truly unified with everything based on the root (/) directory at the top. Do not confuse this root directory that is represented by the forward slash character with the directory actually called "root", which is a subdirectory of the root (/) directory. To avoid confusion in this book the real root directory will always be followed by the forward slash in brackets, and the directory called "root" will have the name in quotation marks.

In Linux the root directory is truly that, and everything else grows out of this directory, as in example directory system of Figure 2.1. Most of these directories are present on the hard drive on which the Linux system is installed. Some of them can actually be other drives or pieces or hardware though. The floppy disc and CD-ROM drives of the system will normally appear in the file structure. In fact they usually appear twice in the file structure, and they are normally to be found in the /mnt (mount) and /dev (device) subdirectories. The files in the /dev directory are used to integrate the drives into the system. If you try writing data to the devices in the /dev directory you could overwrite the existing files making it impossible to use the floppy or CD-ROM drive. Leave this directory alone, and do not experiment with the files it contains. The /mnt directory is where the drives are accessed in the file system, or is where they are "mounted" in Linux terminology. Items of hardware such as modems and the printer are all merged into the file system.

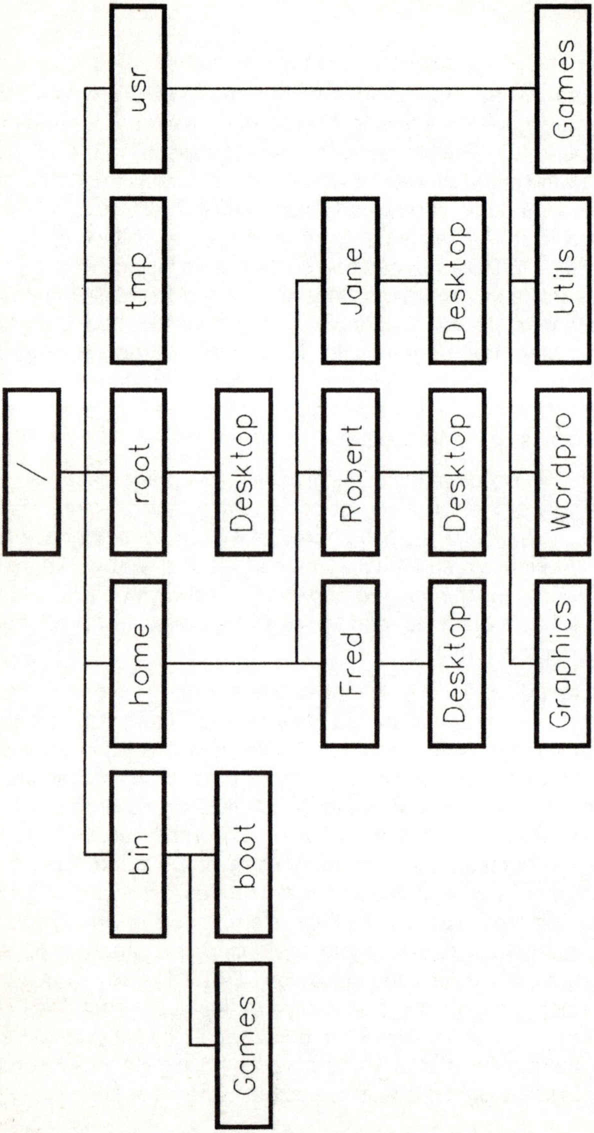

Fig.2.1 An example (and greatly simplified) Linux directory structure

Mounting

Initially the CD-ROM and floppy drives will not be mounted, and this is an area where MS/DOS and Windows work in a much more free and easy manner than Linux. With Windows and MS/DOS you can more or less change discs as and when you please. The system may occasionally complain with an error message when it fails to find the expected disc in the drive, but in general there is unrestricted access to the drives. Linux is much stricter in the way drives having interchangeable discs are handled. Before you can use a drive it must be mounted, and before it can be mounted there must be a disc in the drive, although that disc does not actually have to contain any files. The command used to mount drives is easy to remember, since it is logically called *mount*. What actually has to be typed to mount a given drive depends on the particular set-up of the computer. On the system I am using for these examples the floppy disc drive is accessed at /mnt/floppy, and the CD-ROM is at /mnt/cdrom. You can check the set-up of you Linux system by viewing the file that lists all the mounts in the system. The equivalent of the MS/DOS “type” command in Linux is the “more” command. Type this instruction to view the /etc/fstab file which lists the mounts:

more /etc/fstab

There should be a couple of lines in the file that are similar to these two:

/dev/fd0 /mnt/floppy auto user ,defaults,noauto 0 0

/dev/hdd /mnt/cdrom iso9660 ro,noauto user 0 0

The first line is the one for the floppy drive, and the first two entries on this line show where the floppy drive appears in the file system. Either of these can be used when mounting the drive, so either of these will do the job:

mount /mnt/floppy

mount /dev/fd0

Things operate in a similar manner for the CD-ROM drive, and the first two entries in its section show where it appears in the file system. To mount the CD-ROM drive either of these commands could be used:

mount /mnt/cdrom

mount /dev/hdd

Dismounting

Once a floppy drive or CD-ROM drive has been mounted you should not remove the media until it has been dismounted, or unmounted to use the correct Linux term. In the case of the CD-ROM drive it is unlikely that the eject button on the drive will be operational until the drive has been unmounted. The unmount command follows the same format as the mount command, but the command word *umount* (not unmount) is used instead of mount. These two commands would therefore unmount the floppy and CD-ROM drives:

umount /dev/fd0

umount /mnt/cdrom

Note that you can not unmount a drive if you are actually in that drive at the time, or it is being used in any way by the system. Trying to do so will simply produce an error message indicating that the device is busy.

Navigating

Navigating your way around the file system by way of the command line interpreter is never going to be as easy as using a desktop system such as KDE, and initially it is probably better to experiment with a program such as KDE. However, it is advisable to learn the basics of moving around the file system via the command line interpreter, and navigating around the system in this way is not really that difficult. Apart from some differences caused by the different file structures, moving around a Linux file system is very similar to navigating around an MS/DOS system. If you need to know where you are in the file system the *pwd* (print working directory) command is used. If you try this command it should respond with details of the current directory:

pwd

To move from one directory to another the *cd* (change directory) command is used, and this is similar to the MS/DOS command of the same name. This command would move from the current directory, regardless of which directory it is, to the /usr directory:

cd /usr

It is not necessary to give the full path to the new directory if it a subdirectory of the one that the system is currently in. For example, suppose that you are in the /root directory, and you wish to move to the

/root/Desktop directory. Both of these commands would achieve the desired effect:

cd /root/Desktop

cd Desktop

As in MS/DOS, "." can be used as an abbreviation for the current directory, and ".." can be used as an abbreviation for its parent directory. This command will therefore move one directory higher:

cd ..

For example, if the system was in /root/Desktop when this command was used, it would be in /root afterwards.

Listing

In MS/DOS the *dir* (directory) command is used to list the contents of a directory, and the same command also works with Linux. There is an alternative available in Linux in the form of *ls*, the list command, which seems to be the preferred command for obtaining directory information. Either of these commands will list the contents of the current directory:

ls

dir

The system does not have to be in a directory in order to list its contents. This example will list the contents of the /usr directory regardless of which directory the system happens to be in at the time:

ls /usr

Colour

There is a slight problem with the basic *ls* command in that the information displayed on the screen is rather ambiguous. There is no way of distinguishing between files and subdirectories. With the Linux version of *ls* it is possible to get around this by using the *color* option, as in this example:

ls —color

Note that the word "color" must be spelled the American way, and that using "colour" instead will not work. If you try this on a directory that contains a good selection of files the result should be a colourful display using a different colour for each file type. This list shows the colours used for several common file types:

File Type	Colour
Normal file	White
Program	Green
Directory	Blue
Link	Cyan

I have given the colour of normal files as white, but this colour will be the normal text colour for the display. This will usually be either white or grey. The colour option can be used when listing the contents of something other than the current directory, and the command then takes this form:

ls directory —color

For example, this command would list the contents of the /usr/lib directory in colour:

ls /usr/lib —color

Using this version of the command will also work, because the hyphens in front of the word *color* will ensure that Linux does not interpret it as the directory to be listed:

ls —color /usr/lib

There are other controls that can be used to modify the way in which the *ls* command functions, and you can get brief details of these by using the on-screen help system. To get help on a command simply type the command followed by *—help*, as in this example:

ls —help

Many of the controls enable the list to be sorted in various ways, which can obviously make life easier when dealing with large lists of files. Hidden files are included in the listing if the *-a* switch is used. To have the file size in kilobytes included use both the *-s* and *-k* controls, as in this example:

ls -s -k

You can have the controls as separate entities, as in the above example, but it works just as well in this form, with two or more merged into a single entity:

ls -sk

If you investigate the Linux file system the large number of directories and files may surprise you. To some extent the large number of files is just the way it is done these days, with numerous support files to enable the software to work with disparate items of hardware. It also has to be borne in mind that a typical Linux installation includes more than just the bare fundamentals of the operating system. There may well be dozens of applications programs of various types, including such things as graphics programs, word and text processors, and games.

Directories

Adding and removing directories is handled in much the same way as it is under MS/DOS. New directories are created using the *mkdir* (make directory) command, but note that this can not be abbreviated to an MS/DOS style *md*. This command will produce a subdirectory off the current directory, and it will be called "temp":

mkdir temp

A new directory can be placed anywhere in the file structure by including the full name and path in the command. This example produces a subdirectory called *temp*, and places it off the /root directory:

mkdir /root/temp

The rmdir command is used to remove unwanted directories, but note that this can not be abbreviated to just *rd in* Linux. Also note that a directory can only be removed if it is empty. In this context "empty" means that it must contain no files at all, or subdirectories even if those subdirectories are empty. The *rmdir* command operates in much the same way as the *mkdir* command, and these two examples would remove the directories made using the two *mkdir* examples given previously:

rmdir temp

rmdir /root/temp

Sometimes you may wish to remove a directory, complete with all the files it contains. This can be achieved from the parent directory using the *rm* command and the *-r* (recursive) modifier. The example shown here will remove the directory called "testdir" and all its contents:

rm -r testdir

Obviously great care needs to be taken when deleting files, and even more care must be exercised when removing complete directories.

Files

In the normal course of events users generate files using applications, but for experimental purposes you can generate dummy files using the operating system. This can be achieved using the touch command, as in this example, which would generate a file called "test":

touch test

The file would be placed in the current directory, but it could be placed anywhere in the file structure by including the directory path in addition to the file name. Files can be removed using the *rm* command, and this command would remove the file generated in the previous example.

rm temp

Of course, for this to work the file would have to be in the current directory. By specifying the full path and file name it is possible to remove files in other directories. Depending on the system defaults, you may be asked if you want to remove the file, and you must then reply *y* for yes or *n* for no. There is no built-in file retrieval system, so any files you delete have to be regarded as lost and gone forever.

With MS/DOS it is possible to delete all the files in a directory using the "*" wildcard symbol. This is also possible in Linux, as in this example:

rm /root/*

This will delete all the files in the /root directory, but depending on the default set-up of your system it might be necessary to confirm the removal of each file.

Filenames

Users of MS/DOS will notice that the MS/DOS *.* has been replaced with just * in Linux. MS/DOS filenames can have up to eight characters, plus up to three characters in the extension. The extension follows the main filename, and is separated from it by a full stop. This three-character extension is normally used to indicate the file type, such as ".txt" for a text file or ".jpg" for a JPEG graphics file. Filename extensions can and are used in Linux systems, but the full stop does not have the same significance in Linux as it does in MS/DOS. The full stop character is almost just another character as far as Linux is concerned. The filename "txt.chapter1" is just as valid in Linux as "chapter1.txt", but would obviously not be recognised as a text file by a program that was designed to recognise the "txt" extension. Here are some useful points to remember when thinking up Linux filenames:

Maximum characters

Up to 256 characters can be used in a Linux filename. However, things are much more manageable if you limit yourself to no more than about a dozen.

Case sensitivity

Both upper and lower case letters can be used in filenames, and unlike MS/DOS, Linux regards them as two separate sets of characters. In MS/DOS files called “london”, “LONDON” and “London” would all have the same name, but in Linux they would each have a different name.

Allowable characters

Numbers and most other characters are allowed in filenames, but there are certain characters that should not be used as they have special meanings to the shell and could cause confusing results. These are the characters to avoid:

Ampersand	&
Apostrophe	‘
Asterisk	*
Circumflex	^
Forward slash	/
Hyphen	-
Question mark	?
Quote	“
Vertical bar	|

The space character should also be avoided as the shell might otherwise interpret the filename as two or more filenames separated by spaces.

Wildcards

With some MS/DOS commands it is possible to use wildcards instead of giving a complete filename. Things operate in much the same way with Linux. The asterisk character was used in an earlier example, and this can be used to represent any number of characters. The question mark can be used in place of a single character. Suppose you required a list of the files in a directory that start with “Fig”, this command would list them:

ls Fig*

If you needed to know which files started with “Fig”, had two characters, and then ended with “.gif”, this command would do the job:

ls Fig??.gif

When using the question mark wildcard bear in mind that it will only work if the number of question marks matches up with the number of characters in the filename. For instance, the previous example would match with “Fig12.gif” all right, but it would not match with “Fig1.gif” or “Fig100.gif”. These would both be catered for by this command:

ls Fig*.gif

There is a third wildcard in Linux, which, as far as I am aware, has no equivalent in MS/DOS. The third wildcard is the square bracket, or to be more accurate a pair of square brackets ([]). Suppose you needed to know if there were files called “Fig3.gif”, “Fig4.gif”, and “Fig7.gif”. You could search for specifically for these files using the square brackets and this command:

ls Fig[347].gif

Under most circumstances there is probably no point in using the square brackets, but they can be useful in circumstances where the other wildcards would not be specific enough.

Copying files

Files are copied using the cp command, which must specify the file to be copied and its destination directory. The copy retains the filename of the original. This example would copy the file called “test” from the current directory to the /root directory:

cp test /root

This assumes that the file called “test” is in the current directory. If the source file is not in the current directory the full path must be supplied in addition to the file name, as in this example:

cp /bin/test /root

Use “./” as the destination directory if you wish to copy a file from another directory to the current directory. This command would copy the file called "test" in the /bin directory intoto the current directory.

cp /bin/test ./

The name of the file can be changed during the copy operation, and it is just a matter of giving the new file name when specifying the destination. In this example the file called "nice" in the /bin directory is copied to the current directory as the filed called "bad". Of course, if ./bad was a directory, the file would be copied into this directory under its original name.

cp /bin/nice ./bad

It is possible to copy several files from one directory to another by specifying several source files in the copy command. This command will copy the files called "test" and "test1" from the current directory to the /root directory.

cp test test1 /root

Rather than copying a file you can simply move it using the *mv* instruction. This operates in much the same way as the *cp* command, but the original file is deleted. This command will copy the file called temp in the /usr directory to the current directory, and it will remove the original file.

mv /usr/temp ./

This version of the command has the same effect, but the moved file is renamed "hello" during the move.

mv /usr/tem ./hello

If a complete directory or even a directory structure must be copied, the *cp* command can be used with the *-r* option argument. This example will copy the /usr/test directory, plus all its contents and any subdirectories, to a subdirectory off the current directory. The directory and file names remain unaltered.

cp -r /usr/test ./

An entire directory or directory structure can be moved using the *mv* command, and the *-r* modifier is not needed. This command has the same effect as the previous example, but the original directory structure is removed.

mv /usr/test ./

There would seem to be no Linux equivalent to the MS/DOS diskcopy command, and Linux is less disc oriented than MS/DOS. The contents of a disc can be copied to another disc by roundabout means of course.

This sequence of events will provide the desired result.

Make a temporary directory

Mount the floppy disc

Copy the contents of the disc to the temporary directory

Unmount the floppy disc

Mount the copy disc

Move the contents of the temporary directory to the copy disc

Unmount the copy disc

Remove the temporary directory

This does not give a true clone of the original disc. If you are copying from a system disc, then you must copy to a system disc in order to produce a bootable copy. Copying files from one disc to another is probably easier using KDE and the KFM file manager, which has copy and paste facilities, but it still remains a slightly less than straightforward process.

Renaming

With MS/DOS it is possible to rename files using the *ren* command, but there is no exact equivalent to this in Linux. However, the *mv* command can be used to move the contents of a file to a file of a different name but in the same directory. In other words the file is renamed. This command will take the file in the current directory called "test" and rename it "renamed":

mv ./test ./renamed

This will also work with a directory name, but you need to be very careful when renaming directories. Doing so can render applications or Linux itself unable to locate the files they require.

Reading a file

MS/DOS can be used to read a text file, such as a "readme.txt" file, using the *type* command. The nearest Linux equivalent to this is *cat*, which simply prints a text file on the screen. This command displays the contents of the grops.1 file in the /usr/man/man1 directory:

cat /usr/man/man1/grops.1

The *cat* command is only usable with short files or if you only wish to view the end section of a file. This is due to the fact that it does not give any control over the way the file is displayed, and with a long file most of the text is scrolled off the screen almost instantly. You stand no chance at all of even reading a few words at the beginning of the file. The *less* command is better for large amounts of text, because it displays the file one screen at a time. Simply press the spacebar to move onto the next screen or the Return key to move on one line at a time. In fact there are numerous key controls available. For instance, you can use Control-z or *q* to exit the *less* command, *b* to move up a screen-full and the up and down cursor keys can be used to scroll up and down through the text. However, if you need to view large amounts of text it might be easier to load the file into a "proper" word processor or text editor.

There are two further text-reading commands that are worth mentioning. The *head* command is used to display the beginning of a file, and the *tail* command displays the last few lines. By default ten lines are displayed, but this can be altered using the *-x* control, where *x* is the number of lines to be displayed. These two commands would therefore display the first 20 and last 15 lines in the text file /root/readme:

head -20 /root/readme

tail -15 /root/readme

Links

Earlier in this chapter it was pointed out that the *ls* command can be made to display the names of the main file types in different colours. Link files was one of the file types mentioned, but what exactly is a link file? It is just a link to a file or directory elsewhere on the system, and it provides easier access to that file or directory. This is very much like a *shortcut* in Windows, where (say) an icon on the desktop provides quick access to a program. If you open a link file the result will be the same as if the linked file had been opened. On the face of it, simply moving the file to the directory in which the link is placed would be a better option. In practice this does not always give the desired effect, because the file may only be of use if numerous support files are moved with it. A link provides a quicker and safer way of handing things, because it leaves the file and any support files in place where they should work together properly. Also, with links you can make files accessible from several directories without the need for a copy in each directory.

There are two types of link, which are symbolic links (also known as soft links) and the hard variety. A symbolic link stores the path and file name for the file it links to. If the link is moved or renamed it still points to the file correctly. However, if the file it links to is moved, deleted, or even just renamed, the link will point to nothing. Unless the linked file can be restored a link file containing a broken link should be deleted. For most purposes a symbolic link is all that is needed. A hard link will not be broken if the file it links to is deleted, moved, or renamed. A hard link operates by pointing to the actual data on the disk rather than indirectly via the file name. In effect, the same data has two different file names and paths. Changing one filename still leaves the other one pointing to the right data on the disc. Many links are added into the file system when Linux is installed.

Links are produced using the *ln* command, and to produce a soft link the *-s* option is used. A hard link is produced by default. These two example produce hard and soft links in the current directory to a file called "readme" in the /usr directory. In both cases the link is called "readlink".

ln /usr/readme readlink

ln -s /usr/readme readlink

Note that the name of the file being linked comes first, followed by the name of the link.

Running programs

In order to run a program under MS/DOS you can either go into the directory that contains the program file and type the name of the file, or you can type in the full path and name of the file to run it from any directory. The full path approach will work with Linux, but going into the appropriate directory and typing the file name will not necessarily do so. This depends on the version of Linux you are using. However, if the program name is preceded by "./" it will certainly run. These two examples would run the program called "klondike" in the /usr/bin directory. The first will work from any directory and the second requires the system to be in the /usr/bin directory.

/usr/bin/klondke

./klondike

Remember that programs can be run via link files if desired.

Keeping tabs

If you are used to the "point and-click" approach of a graphical user interface such as Windows, a text-based environment such as a Linux console is going to be tough going. Some Linux shells, including *bash*, provide a certain amount of help by automatically completing commands when the Tab key is pressed. For this to work it has to be possible for the computer to work out what comes next with absolute certainty. On one of my Linux computers if I type the first line of text shown here and then press the Tab key, the computer adds text to produce the second line.

cd /d

cd /dev/

It can do this because there is only one directory off the root directory that has a name starting with the letter "d". Consequently, the computer knows that what comes next must be "ev/". It does not know whether or not you wish to go further down into the directory structure so it stops there and awaits further input from the user. If there were two directories off the root directory starting with the letter "d" the computer would be stumped and would indicate so by producing a warning "beep". You can then try pressing the Alt key, and provided what has been typed so far is correct, the computer will display a list of all the possible endings to the command. This does not only work on paths and file names incidentally. If you type in this:

shu

Pressing the Tab key will result in the computer adding text to produce this:

shutdown

There is only one command that starts with "shu", so the computer knows that you require the *shutdown* command. It can not add any option controls for you though as it can not mind-read, and if any of these are required they must be added manually.

Virtual consoles

Linux has a virtual console facility that enables up to six consoles to be used. In order to change to a new console simple press the Alt key simultaneously with one of function keys one to six. At start-up you log into console number one, so to switch to a new console you must use function keys two to six. You have to log in again on the new console, but you do not have to log in as a different user. Of course, you only have to log in to a console the first time you switch to it. Thereafter in the session you can move straight from one console to another. This gives a form of multi-tasking where you can have (say) a word processor operating on one console and a game on the other. If the boss arrives on the scene you can almost instantly switch from the game back to the word processor. Of course, as with any form of multi-tasking the demands on the computer are increased as more programs are run. In particular, memory requirements tend to increase dramatically as the number of consoles and applications in use are increased. With a PC that has a limited amount of memory this factor might restrict the use of multiple consoles.

When you have finished using a virtual console the logout command can be used to switch it off. Pressing the Alt key and a suitable function key then takes the system into another console. You do not actually have to logout of unused consoles, and they can be left running while you use another console. When the system is shutdown, all active consoles will be terminated “cleanly”. However, a console left running unnecessarily will presumably waste system resources, and should therefore be shutdown.

Rebooting

As we saw in the previous chapter, the system can be shutdown “cleanly” and immediately using this command:

shutdown -h now

The *shutdown* command will only work if you login as “root” incidentally. Without root privileges it simply generates an error message. Like Windows, you should not simply terminate a session by switching off the computer. This would leave files open and could produce problems the next time the computer is used. Also, the next time Linux is used it will detect that it was not shut down properly, and it will go through a lengthy check of the hard disc drive before booting-up properly.

There are two options available if a reboot of the computer is required. The easiest way is to simultaneously press the Control, Alt, and Delete keys, which is the same method used in MS/DOS. The alternative is to use this version of the shutdown command:

shutdown -r now

The *-r* option tells the computer to reboot, whereas the *-h* option used in the previous example tells the computer to halt once it has shutdown. The *now* option in both examples tells Linux to execute the command at once, which is what you normally require when Linux on a workstation. The alternative is to use a time here.

Text editing

Under the later versions of MS/DOS it is possible to produce and edit text files using the *edit* command. This is useful for editing files such as the autoexec.bat and config.sys files. You may also find it necessary to produce or edit files under Linux. In fact you almost certainly will. You may prefer to go into X Windows and use one of the "X" text editors that are available. This is certainly my preferred way of handling things. If you prefer to use a traditional text editor there should be both *Emacs* and *Vi* available on the system. *Emacs* seems to be generally regarded the more accomplished of the two but they are both capable of handling large text files if necessary. To edit a file called /root/hello using *Emacs* and *Vi* these commands would be used:

emacs /root/hello

vi /root/hello

Note that it may be *Xemacs* rather than *Emacs* that runs if you are using a console from within an X Windows front-end such as KDE. If this should happen, exit to the console in order to run *Emacs*.

In order to edit an exiting file it is just a matter of including the path and name of the file in the command. For example, these commands would open an existing file called /root/goodbye:

emacs /root/goodbye

vi /root/goodbye

Incidentally, with a modern version of Linux the *vi* command will actually run an improved version of *vi* called *vim* by way of a link. Neither of these text edits are much like the MS/DOS "edit" program, but *Emacs* is probably the easier program to use if you are used to *edit* or a similar MS/DOS text editor. Try making a test file by typing in this command:

emacs /root/testing

Once into the *Emacs* editor you can type some text, use the cursor keys to move around the text, and delete text using the Delete and Backspace keys. Text can be freely added into the middle of existing text. With MS/DOS and Windows text editors it is normally possible to toggle between the insert and overwrite modes by toggling the Insert key. Unfortunately this does not work with *Emacs* (or other Linux software), and pressing the Insert key simply produces a warning "beep". I do not know if there is an overwrite mode, but I have never found a way of switching into it. Once you have completed the test file you can save the file by pressing Control-x followed by Control-s. Virtually all *Emacs* commands require the user to simultaneously press the Control key and one other, or the Meta key plus another key. In a PC context the Meta key is usually the Alt key but might be the Escape key. Some commands, as in this example, require a sequence of two pairs of key presses. To exit *Emacs* use the Control-x and Control-c sequence. The *less* command can then be used to check that the file exists and that its contents are correct.

The list of available *Emacs* commands is huge, but for producing and editing small to medium size text files you can get away with using just a few of them. This is a list of some of the more important *Emacs* commands.

Save

Control-x Control-s	Saves to disc
Control-x Control-w	Save as
Alt z	Save text to disc and exit

Open

Control-x Control-f	Open
Control-x Control-r	Opens file which replaces the contents of the current buffer
Control-x Control-i	opens file and inserts it at the current cursor position

Cursor

Control-f	Move forward one character
Control-b	Move backward one character
Control-a	Move to beginning of line
Control-e	Move to end of line
Control-n	Move to next line
Control-p	Move to previous line

Delete/Insert

Control-c	Insert a space character
Control-d	Delete next character
Alt d	Delete next word
Control-k	Delete to end of line
Return	Insert a new line

Adding users

Linux is, of course, a multi-user system, and it is possible to have a large number of users share the same computer. This is a subject that is covered in more detail in chapter 4, and here we will only cover the addition of users to the system. At least one user account must be started during the installation process, and this is the "root" account for the superuser. The "root" account has complete access to the system and can make drastic changes to the system. For this reason due care has to be exercised when logged in as "root", or the system could be inadvertently trashed. The normal way of handling things is to login as "root" when changes must be made to the system, but to login as a normal user at other times, even if you are the only person who will use the computer.

There may be an opportunity to add users during the installation process, and if this should be the case I would advise adding at lease one user (you) at this stage. In fact it is a good time to add any other user accounts that will be needed. If you should need to add further accounts later on it can be done from the command line using the *adduser* command. This command is included in most typical installations, but it might be necessary to add it to the installation if you have installed some form of minimal installation. Note that the *adduser* command is only available when you are logged in as "root". To add a user called "Fred" you would use this command:

adduser Fred

Linux will respond with several lines of text, which should look something like this:

Looking for first available UID... 501

Looking for first available GID... 500

Adding login: Fred...done.

Creating home directory: /home/Fred...done.

Creating mailbox: /var/spool/mail/Fred...done.

Don't forget to set the password.

This tells you that the Linux has found the next available user identity (UID) and group identity (GID) numbers, which it has used, and that it has added the name Fred to the login process. It has also produced directories that will be needed by the new user. The last line reminds you that the password for the new user must be set, otherwise it will not be possible for "Fred" to login. To set or change a password the *passwd* command is used. Suppose that we wish to set the password for the "Fred" account as "hello". To get the process underway this command would be used:

passwd Fred

Note that you must be logged in as "root" for this to work. You will be asked for the new password, and having typed it in once you will then be asked to repeat the process. This is simply to ensure that you have not made a mistake when typing it in for the first time. As usual, the password will not be displayed on the screen so that it is difficult for any onlookers to see what you are typing. To set the password as "hello" you would therefore type in this:

hello

hello

Having set the password for the "Fred" account it should then be possible to login as "Fred" using the "hello" password. In order to change a password you simply login as the appropriate user and then issue this command:

passwd

When prompted you must supply the old password, followed by the new password twice. The new password is then in operation and must be used whenever a password is required for that user. I suppose *passwd* could be regarded as a command "with attitude", because it will not accept passwords that it considers to be too simple or obvious. If it will not accept your first attempt you must try again, and keep trying until it does accept you choice of password.

Tar

When using Linux you are likely to encounter *tar* files before too long. These are tape archive files, and the *tar* command is primarily intended as a simple backup facility. The basic action of the *tar* command is to take a group of files and merge them into one long file. The same program can be used to restore the original files. Modern versions of this program can also compress the files so that they require less storage space. This command is more or less the Linux equivalent of a MS/DOS or Windows ZIP compression program.

Modern computing tends to deal more in gigabytes than in megabytes, and comprehensive backing up is not practical unless your computer is equipped with some form of mass storage device that can read and write data and has interchangeable media. This used to be some form of tape backup system, but these days is more likely to be some form of interchangeable disc such as a ZIP or CDR. Without such a device fitted to your PC the only option is to backup data to floppy discs when each file is produced. In the event that the system becomes trashed it is a matter of installing and setting it up again from scratch, although it should be possible to make backups of system files. Although more time consuming, I would be inclined to simply set up everything from scratch, and take the opportunity to start again with a "clean" system.

Even if you do not use *tar* files for backup purposes, you will almost certainly have to deal with them from time to time. Programs are often distributed in the form of *tar* files. Apparently Linux filenames can give problems with other systems, as they can contain characters that are not allowed by other operating systems. They can also be longer than most other operating systems will allow. It is quite likely that there will be problems if you try to download a group of Linux files on a non-Linux system and put them onto a CD-ROM so that they can be transferred to a Linux system. If the files are downloaded in the form of a single *tar* file having a simple filename there should be no problems. Provided the storage media can handle it properly, dealing with one large file is often more convenient than dealing with large numbers of files anyway.

The *tar* program is reasonably simple to use, but matters are complicated somewhat by the large number of options available. The command takes this form:

tar options tar-file source

For full details of the options available refer to the online manual. These are just some of the options available:

c Create new archive

f Place archive on a file or device

r Append new files to existing archive

t List the names of files in an archive

v Verbose (list filenames as they are added or extracted)

x Extract files from an archive

M Expect multi-volume archive

W Verify that archive does not contain errors

Z Compress or uncompress (zip) files

For the sake of this example assume that you wish to archive the files in /root/temp to a floppy disc. First the floppy disc drive must be fitted with a disc having sufficient storage space, and then it must be mounted. This command would then have the desired effect, archiving the files to a single file called "bu1.tar":

tar cfv /mnt/floppy/bu1.tar /root/temp

The *c* option tells tar to create a new archive, the *f* option instructs it to put the archive in a file, and the *v* option gets tar to place messages on the screen showing exactly what it is doing. The *v* is optional, but the *c* and *f* are essential.

Zipping

To do the same thing but compress the files in the archive the *Z* option would be added, as shown here:

tar cfvZ /mnt/floppy/bu1.tar /root/temp

The *Z* has not been put in uppercase by mistake. Some option letters have different functions depending on whether they are in upper or lower case, so as usual with Linux you have to be careful to use the right one. The usual hyphen ahead of the options has also been omitted, and these options will not function if it is included. If you get things wrong it is possible that *tar* will hang-up. If this should happen, using the Control-z key combination should restore control.

To produce a list of files in this zipped archive the following command would be used:

tar ftZ /mnt/floppy/bu1.tar

The "Z" must be included or *tar* will not recognise the file as a valid *tar* file, and will return an error message. Of course, to read the contents of the non-zipped version the Z would have to be omitted for the same reason.

Multi-volume

With the *tar* program it is possible to archive files to a device rather than a file. In other words you specify a device such as the floppy drive as the destination rather than a file. To do this the device must first be mounted of course. Suppose that the /root/temp directory is to be archived on floppy disc. First the floppy drive would be mounted using a command such as this:

mount /dev/fd0

A blank floppy disc to take the archive should be placed in the drive before the mount command is issued. This command would then be used to make the archive on the floppy disc:

tar cfv /dev/fd0 /root/temp

The relatively low capacity of a floppy disc is a definite drawback when backing up directories, because the amount of data in the directory may well be several times greater than the capacity of a single floppy disc. Even with a higher capacity drive it may still be necessary to backup more data than a single tape or disc can accommodate. Some MS/DOS and Windows archive programs get around this problem by enabling an archive file to be spread across several discs or tapes. The MS/DOS *Arj* program and the recent versions of *Winzip* have this ability. Fortunately, so does the Linux *tar* program. Archives that are too large for one disc or tape are not automatically spread across several volumes, and the "M" option must be used in the tar command. This is the multi-volume version of the previous example:

tar cfvM /dev/fd0 /root/temp

The program will tell you when to change to the next disc in the set. The discs should be numbered so that you can use them in the correct order when restoring files.

Restoring

Since they are archived into a single file, the files backed up using *tar* are not directly usable. The files must be extracted, and this is done using the *tar* program again. The command for extracting files is actually much the same as the one for producing them in the first place, but the "x" (extract) option is used in place of the "c" (create) option. A command to extract the files from an archive takes this form:

tar options archive destination

The destination is optional, and if it is not specified the files will be placed into the current directory. This command would reverse an earlier example, and take the files from bu1.tar on a floppy disc and place them in /root/temp:

tar xfv /mnt/floppy/bu1.tar /root/temp

There is a potential trap here in that *tar* removes the leading "/" from filenames, and when files are restored they do not have absolute names. This does not matter provided you go into the root (/) directory before restoring files using *tar*. In other words, use this command:

cd /

Otherwise the files in this example would be placed in /root/temp off the current directory. Another way around this is to not use absolute paths when archiving files using *tar*. This command would archive the files in the current directory to file "bu1.tar" on the floppy disc:

tar cvf /mnt/floppy/bu1.tar *

This would extract the files and place them back in the current directory:

tar xvf /mnt/floppy/bu1.tar *

Note that it is not just files that *tar* archives, and any subdirectories and their contents will be treated as part of the directory being archived.

Extracting files from a device is much the same as extracting them from a file, but the device rather than a file is specified as the source. This example would reverse the example of archiving to a device given previously:

tar xvf /dev/fd0 /root/temp

With multi-volume archives the "M" option must be included, as in this example:

tar xvfM /dev/fd0 /root/temp

The correct floppy discs must be inserted in the drive when requested by the program, and you will be in trouble if they were not numbered when the archive was created!

Tar is undoubtedly a rather complex program to use, but for some simple file archiving it should not cause too many difficulties. There are plenty of clever features available if you wish to use it in a more sophisticated fashion, and it is well worthwhile reading through the on-line documentation. Incidentally, if you write to a floppy disc as a device rather than as a file using *tar* you will find that the disc is no longer usable as an ordinary disc. In order to use it again as a standard disc it will have to be formatted which will, of course, remove any data it contains.

RPM

Many programs are distributed as *tar* files, or more usually zipped *tar* files. In order to use one of these the files are extracted into a directory on the hard disc, and then the readme file is read to determine what to do next. This will often entail running an installation program, but the included documentation should give concise instructions on how to get the software "up and running". The main alternative to *tar* files is the RPM variety. RPM in this context stands for Red Hat Package Manager, and although this software was produced by Red Hat it is freely usable and any recent version of Linux should be equipped to deal with this type of file. You will often find that you have the option of installing software from some form of *tar* file or a RPM type. RPM files have definite advantages, so given the choice it is almost certainly better to opt for the RPM route.

At first sight there may seem to be no need for RPM or any form of package installation program. Why not simply load a program file onto the hard disc and run it? This type of thing was the norm in the days of MS/DOS and other relatively simple operating systems, but few programs these days are truly in the stand-alone category. Most programs rely heavily on support files, some of which are unique to a particular program. Many of these support files are used by a number of programs though, and it is these shared files that tend to cause problems with modern computer systems. In many ways computing life would be much easier if every program came complete with all the files it required, with the program being installed complete with those files into its own directory. The problem with this approach is that there would be a great deal of duplication and wasted disc space.

The drawback of the shared approach and each program being dependent on support files is that there is plenty of opportunity for things to go wrong. If a program requires certain files to be present on the computer are those files already installed? If the required files are already present, are they the correct versions? RPM is designed to ensure that loading new software or upgrading existing programs does not cause problems. If some of the required support files are not already present on the computer or included in the program files, RPM will point out the problem and prevent installation until the missing files are installed. If the source files include one that is the same as a file already on the computer but an older version, RPM will prevent the newer file from being overwritten. This should ensure that adding new software does not prevent existing programs from running properly. It is probably impossible to produce a system that will guarantee a perfect installation every time, but RPM greatly reduces the risk of things going seriously wrong.

Installation

RPM can be used via a graphical front-end, and you may prefer to use it via KDE, but it is not difficult to use it from the command line. Note that you will probably have to login as "root" in order to use RPM, since its use obviously involves changes to the system. To install a package using RPM use this command:

rpm -i package-name

If all is well, RPM will install the software plus any support files and documentation included in the package. If RPM detects that all is not well it will not proceed and will produce an error message explaining what has gone wrong. This is most likely to be where the package you are trying to install is dependent on another package being present on the computer, but this other package is absent. The new package is of no use without this other package, which must be obtained and installed first. RPM should then be able to install the new package without any problems. It is actually possible to force RPM to install the software anyway using the *—nodeps* option, but doing so is pointless. The installed software would not run properly and could hang-up the computer.

If RPM indicates that it can not install the package without overwriting a file or files belonging to another package, you can force it to do so if you wish. It is just a matter of using this version of the command, but forcing an overwrite of other files is a little risky:

rpm -i —replacefiles package-name

A lot of software is loaded onto the hard disc during a typical Linux installation, so having taken the time to locate a program you may occasionally find that RPM informs you it is already on the system! If you select a large Linux installation it is worthwhile checking through the menus and the file system to determine exactly what has been installed. This could save a great deal of wasted time and effort later.

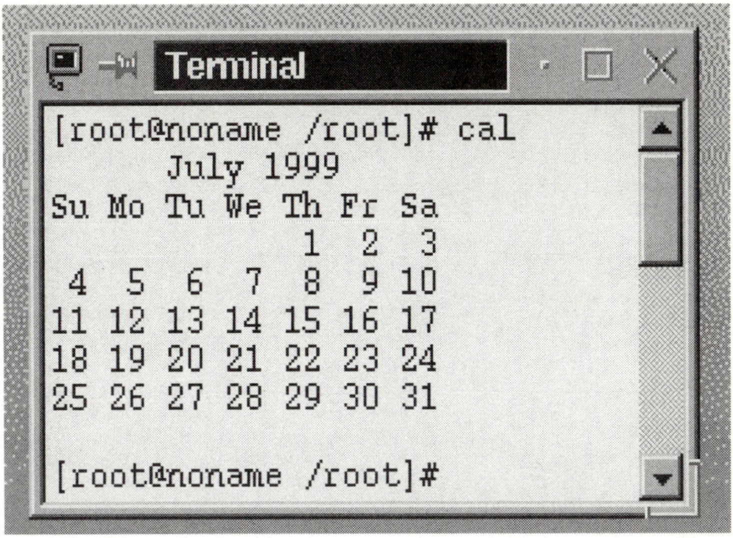

Fig.2.2 A simple one-month calendar produced by the cal command

Upgrading

The upgrade command is similar to the one for installing software "from scratch", but the upgrade (*-U*) option is used instead of the install (*-i*) option. This is the upgrade version of the RPM command:

rpm -U packagename

RPM can be used to uninstall programs, and it is just a matter of using the erase (*-e*) option in the command:

rpm -e programname

Here the name used in the command is the name of the program file, and not the name of the file that was used during installation (which will have numerous characters in addition to the basic name).

Extras

There are a number of useful little extra facilities available from the Linux command line, and one of these is the *cal* (calendar) command. In its most basic form you simply type this command:

cal

```
[root@noname /root]# cal 2001
                               2001

       January               February                 March
Su Mo Tu We Th Fr Sa   Su Mo Tu We Th Fr Sa   Su Mo Tu We Th Fr Sa
    1  2  3  4  5  6                1  2  3                1  2  3
 7  8  9 10 11 12 13    4  5  6  7  8  9 10    4  5  6  7  8  9 10
14 15 16 17 18 19 20   11 12 13 14 15 16 17   11 12 13 14 15 16 17
21 22 23 24 25 26 27   18 19 20 21 22 23 24   18 19 20 21 22 23 24
28 29 30 31            25 26 27 28            25 26 27 28 29 30 31

        April                   May                   June
Su Mo Tu We Th Fr Sa   Su Mo Tu We Th Fr Sa   Su Mo Tu We Th Fr Sa
 1  2  3  4  5  6  7          1  2  3  4  5                   1  2
 8  9 10 11 12 13 14    6  7  8  9 10 11 12    3  4  5  6  7  8  9
15 16 17 18 19 20 21   13 14 15 16 17 18 19   10 11 12 13 14 15 16
22 23 24 25 26 27 28   20 21 22 23 24 25 26   17 18 19 20 21 22 23
29 30                  27 28 29 30 31         24 25 26 27 28 29 30

        July                  August                September
Su Mo Tu We Th Fr Sa   Su Mo Tu We Th Fr Sa   Su Mo Tu We Th Fr Sa
 1  2  3  4  5  6  7             1  2  3  4                      1
 8  9 10 11 12 13 14    5  6  7  8  9 10 11    2  3  4  5  6  7  8
15 16 17 18 19 20 21   12 13 14 15 16 17 18    9 10 11 12 13 14 15
22 23 24 25 26 27 28   19 20 21 22 23 24 25   16 17 18 19 20 21 22
29 30 31               26 27 28 29 30 31      23 24 25 26 27 28 29
                                              30
       October               November               December
Su Mo Tu We Th Fr Sa   Su Mo Tu We Th Fr Sa   Su Mo Tu We Th Fr Sa
    1  2  3  4  5  6                1  2  3                      1
 7  8  9 10 11 12 13    4  5  6  7  8  9 10    2  3  4  5  6  7  8
14 15 16 17 18 19 20   11 12 13 14 15 16 17    9 10 11 12 13 14 15
21 22 23 24 25 26 27   18 19 20 21 22 23 24   16 17 18 19 20 21 22
28 29 30 31            25 26 27 28 29 30      23 24 25 26 27 28 29
                                              30 31
```

Fig.2.3 The cal command can also produce a calendar for a year

By default this command produces a calendar for the current month. Figure 2.2 shows an example calendar produced using this command. You can specify the month and year if you require the calendar for something other than the current month. This command will print a calendar for June 2002:

cal 6 2002

It is important to give the year in full, and not to give just the last two digits (e.g. "99" for "1999"). If you do this you will get a calendar for the year 99, and not the year 1999! A calendar for a whole year can be produced, and it is just a matter of specifying the year in the command, but no month. This command will produce a calendar for the year 2001 (Figure 2.3).

cal 2001

Locating files

Linux has more than one file finding utility, some of which are easier to use than others. The *locate* command is relatively quick and easy to use. Its speed is due to the program keeping a database of files on the hard disc, so when it searches for a file it searches the database and not the hard disc itself. For this command to work it must obviously have a database to work from, and the database is produced and then updated automatically at about 6.00 AM. You have to bear in mind here that Linux has its origins in the world of large computers that run more or less continuously. Obviously this automatic generation and update facility will not work if you PC runs "from nine to five", or at random times during the day. However, the database can be produced manually or updated using this command:

/usr/bin/updatedb

It will take a minute or so for this task to complete, but once it has done so you should be able to locate files by name quite quickly. You must login as root to produce the database, but once it has been generated any user can utilize the *locate* command. To locate a file you simply issue the *locate* command and include the filename, as in this example:

locate convert

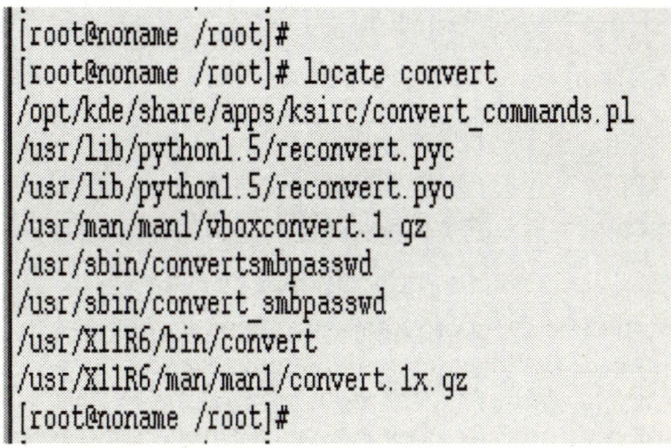

```
[root@noname /root]#
[root@noname /root]# locate convert
/opt/kde/share/apps/ksirc/convert_commands.pl
/usr/lib/python1.5/reconvert.pyc
/usr/lib/python1.5/reconvert.pyo
/usr/man/man1/vboxconvert.1.gz
/usr/sbin/convertsmbpasswd
/usr/sbin/convert_smbpasswd
/usr/X11R6/bin/convert
/usr/X11R6/man/man1/convert.1x.gz
[root@noname /root]#
```

Fig.2.4 Example output from the locate command

The *locate* command will respond with any filenames that include the text string you use, and this might result in several files being suggested. With this example command my computer responded with a list of eight files (Figure 2.4), because it located files called "reconvert" for instance. However, it is not usually too difficult to identify the one you require from the list provided. Unfortunately, wildcards can not be used in the locate command.

Date and time

The *date* command enables the date and time to be read, and also permits the time to be set by the "root" user. To get the computer to print the time and date on the screen you simply issue the straightforward *date* command:

date

It will then respond with something like this:

Sun Jul 18 22 : 54 : 23 BST 1999-07-18

There are numerous formatting options available that can be used to print the time in 12-hour format and this type of thing. These options are used by adding "+" and the appropriate formatting string at the end of the command. This list gives some of the formatting strings and their functions.

String	**Function**
%a	Abbreviated day only
%A	Full day only
%b	Abbreviated month only
%B	Full month only
%D	mm/dd/yy format for date
%H	24-hour format with leading zeros
%I	12-hour format with leading zeros
%k	24-hour format with no leading zeros
%j	Print the number of the day in the year (001 to 366)

%I	12-hour format with no leading zeros
%M	Minutes only
%p	AM/PM only
%r	12-hour format with AM/PM
%U	Print week number of year (01 to 53)
%Y	Year only
%Z	Time zone only

This command would print the year:

date %Y

This example would print the full name of the month and whether it is AM or PM:

date +“%B %p”

The month and AM/PM options are enclosed in quotation marks (with no space between the plus sign and the first quotation mark), and a space is inserted between them. This results in a space between the two pieces of data when they are printed on the screen. Any desired text characters can be used as separators, and in this version of the command a comma and a space will be placed between the month and the AM/PM indication.

date +“%B, %p”

Setting the date

The system clock is set using the date command in this form:

date MM/DD/hh/mm/YYYY

MM is the month and is a two-digit number from 01 to 12

DD is the day and is a two-digit number from 01 to 31

hh is the hour in 24-hour format and is from 00 to 23 (00 is midnight)

mm is the minutes and is a two digit number from 00 to 59

YYYY is the year in full four-digit format

It is not possible to specify the seconds, which are set at zero when the command is used. This command will set the date and time to 7 : 23 PM (19 : 23) on the 16th February 2002:

date 021619232002

Of course, a command such as this that affects the system will only work if the "root" user issues it. It is important to realise that the *date* command does not alter the PC's hardware clock, and what it is really doing is adjusting the data read from the clock to give the specified time and date. Where a computer is left running continuously this does not matter, and the time and date read from the hardware clock will be adjusted accordingly, and apart from any drift in the clock will be correct. If the computer is rebooted the time and date will be taken direct from the hardware clock, and no offset will then be applied unless a suitable *date* command is used again. For most PC users it is therefore better to correct the time and date by going into the BIOS Setup program and correcting the hardware clock. The correct time and date will then be obtained even if the computer is switched off and rebooted.

Word count

There are a number of commands concerned with text files, but these are not necessarily of real use in a modern computing context. There are applications programs that can handle most of these functions in a more user-friendly fashion. One that might be of use is the unfortunately named *wc* (word count in this context) command. If you wished to know the number of words in a text file called /root/chap1.txt this command would provide the answer:

wc /root/chap1.txt

This would actually produce a response such as this from the computer:

```
321   10726   60403   /root/chap1.txt
```

When used without any flags this command actually tells you slightly more than the number of words in the file. From left to right the three figures are the number of lines, words, and text characters. This file therefore contains 10726 words. Use the appropriate option or options from this list if you only require one or two parameters.

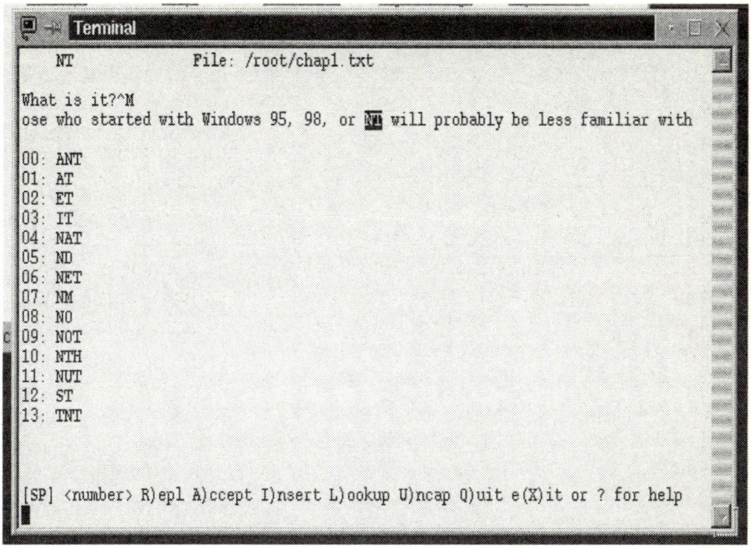

Fig.2.5 The ispell correction window in action

Option	**Parameter**
-c	Number of characters (Bytes)
-l	Number of lines
-w	Number of words

Ispell

Ispell is the Linux interactive spell-checker, which integrates with some text editors but can also be used from the command line. To use it from the command line simply issue the command followed by the filename of the file to be checked. To check the file called /root/chap1.txt this command would be used:

ispell /root/chap1.txt

An interactive screen offers several options if an error is found (Figure 2.5). The top line shows the word that is being queried and the name of the file being checked. The line of text containing the suspect word is shown beneath that, so that you can see the context in which the word occurs. Beneath that there is a list of suggested corrections, if *ispell* can find words in its dictionary that are similar to the word that is being queried. At the bottom of the screen there is a line of text that lists the options available to you. If you wish to use one of the suggested replacements simply type in its number and press the Return key. The look-up option enables the dictionary to be searched for a word or search string containing wildcards, and a list of matches is then provided (Figure 2.6). With the replace option you can type in a word to replace the existing word. For a brief explanation of the various options type "?" and press the Return key to bring up a help screen. For a command line utility *ispell* is remarkably good, and it rivals the spell-checking facilities built into many up-market word processors.

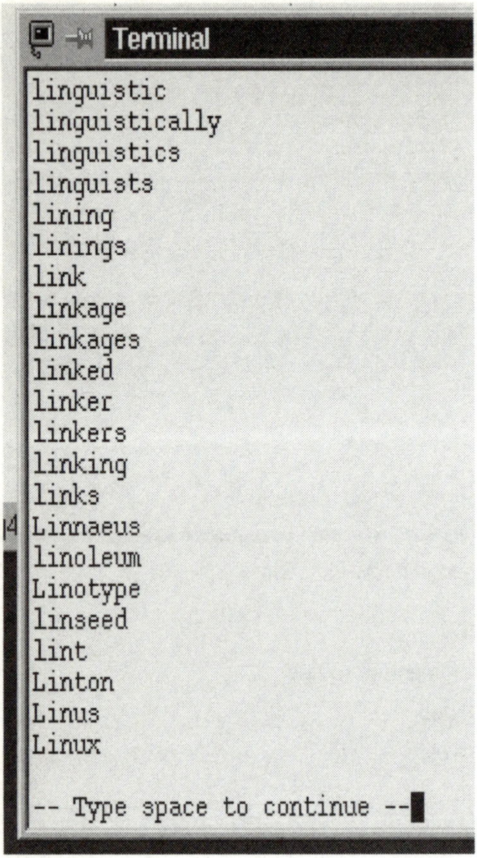

Fig.2.6 The ispell lookup facility in action

Correcting

One potential drawback of a command line interpreter is that if a mistake is made it can be necessary to retype a long and complex command. This is not necessary with MS/DOS where pressing function key three (F3) results in the last command appearing on the screen. If you make a mistake and get an error message it is just a matter of pressing F3 to bring up the incorrect version of the command, editing it with the aid of the cursor keys plus the Insert and Delete keys, and then pressing the

Enter key. Similar facilities are available at the Linux command line, but pressing F3 will not bring up the last command again. Instead, press the up cursor key to resurrect the last command. Pressing the down cursor key will clear the command line again. The left and right cursor keys move the cursor so that corrections can be made. The Insert key is unlikely to be operative, and the command line interpreter is permanently in an equivalent of the MS/DOS "insert" mode. In other words, anything typed at the keyboard will be added into the existing text and will not overwrite it. The Backspace and Delete keys should be operative, but you will probably find that the Delete key simply duplicates the Backspace function. However, this is all you need in order to edit commands.

With MS/DOS it is possible to clear the console screen and start afresh at the top using the *cls* command. This is the Linux equivalent:

clear

This will of course produce the usual prompt at the top of the screen, and not a totally blank screen.

Equivalents

This list gives the Linux equivalents to common MS/DOS commands, and provides a quick reference source for those trying to make the move from MS/DOS to Linux.

MS/DOS	**Linux**
cd path	cd path
cd \	cd /
cd ..	cd ..
cls	clear
Control-Alt-Del	Control-Alt-Del or shutdown -r now
copy	cp
date	date
del filename	rm filename
del *.*	rm *
dir	dir or ls
diskcopy	No direct equivalent

format	Use KDE and KFloppy to format floppy discs
md	mkdir
rd	rmdir
ren	mv filename new-filename
Time	Date
type filename	less filename (Control -z to exit)

More useful commands

Alt-F1 to F6	Change console
adduser	Add a new user
cal	Prints a calendar for the current month
cal month year	Prints a calendar for the specified month
cal year	Prints a calendar for the specified year
date	Print the current time and date
ispell filename	Spell check a text file
ln file/folder linkname	Create a hard link
ln -s file/folder linkname	Create a soft link
mount	mount a device
mv filename directory	Move the named file to the named path or directory
passwd	Enables current user to change their password
passwd name	Enables root user to change a password
pwd	Show current path/directory
rm -r directory name	Remove a folder plus any files or folders it contains
shutdown -h now	Shutdown Linux immediately
tar cfv filename folder	Archive the folder and its contents in the named file

tar cfvZ filename folder	Zipped version of above
tar xfv filename folder	Unarchive files in specified file to specified folder
tar xfvZ filename folder	Unzip version of above
umount	unmount a device
wc	Word count (provides the number of words, lines and characters in a text document

Note that some of these commands are only possible if the user has root privileges.

3

Using KDE

A Linux GUI

The Linux command interpreter has a wide range of commands, and it can be programmed to make light work of complex and repetitive tasks. It is undoubtedly very powerful, but like any command line interpreter it does not score well in terms of user-friendliness. These days most users prefer a graphical user interface, and will not settle for anything less. Linux has more than one graphical user interface to choose from, but the K Desktop Environment, which is normally just called KDE, is the one that is most widely used. This is included with most Linux distributions, and is central to some of them, particularly Caldera Open Linux. Superficially KDE looks a bit like a 32-bit version of Windows, and with the latest version you can select a Windows look to the desktop if you like. BEOS and Mac flavours of the desktop are also on offer.

However, below the surface KDE is significantly different to Windows, or any other operating system. You can select a Windows, BEOS, or Mac look to the desktop, but KDE still operates in more or less standard KDE fashion. For someone used to any other graphical user interface there is a certain amount of learning to do before getting fully in control of things. On the other hand, with a little experimentation you can soon start to find your way around the system, and undertake a few basic tasks. If you are not familiar with the Linux file system life will be very difficult until you have learnt the general scheme of things used by Linux. Before getting too deeply into KDE it is necessary to read the parts of the previous chapter that deal with the Linux directory structure. Setting up and using KDE should then be reasonably pain-free.

Versions

Like everything else in the world of computing, KDE is gradually evolving. At the time of writing this there are only two versions of KDE, which are versions 1.0 and 1.1. The latter is quite new, but should soon take over from version 1.0. Obviously you must have KDE installed on your PC in order to work your way through the material in this chapter. KDE 1.1 is preferable, and if possible installations equipped with version 1.0 should be upgraded. Most of the material provided here is relevant to both versions, and where necessary any large differences between the two versions are pointed out.

With some Linux distributions KDE is run automatically once Linux has booted-up, but with most it is necessary to run it from the command line editor. To do this it is just a matter of logging in as usual and then using this command:

kde

The program may be called KDE, but in order to run it you must type "kde" rather than "KDE". The two versions are very similar in operation, but there are some important differences. One of these becomes apparent when you first run KDE. With version 1.0 you go straight into the KDE desktop, but the first time you run version 1.1 a Windows style wizard provides some initial help in getting things set up for immediate use. As pointed out previously, one of these is to set the look of the desktop to standard KDE, Windows, BEOS, or Mac OS. This can be easily changed at any time, but initially I would suggest that you settle for the standard KDE look.

Another difference is that version 1.1 will optionally add icons for the floppy disc or discs to the desktop, plus an icon for the CD-ROM. I would suggest that you let KDE add icons for these, as the icons make it much easier to deal with the floppy drive or drives and the CD-ROM drive. If you are using version 1.0 it is advisable to add icons for these drives at an early stage. This is covered in the section of this chapter that deals with the use of disc drives.

The desktop

Once into KDE the screen should look something like Figure 3.1. If you have used any form of windowing environment the KDE desktop should look slightly familiar, but there are some aspects that will not.

Trash

The Trash icon is equivalent to the Trashcan in some operating systems, and the Recycling Bin in Windows. The icons representing files can be dragged to the Trash icon and dropped there to delete them. This is the KDE equivalent of the command line *rm* (remove) command, but like the Windows Recycle Bin files are not destroyed when they are dropped into the Trash icon. They are moved from their original location into a

Fig.3.1 The KDE desktop with no windows open

directory for deleted files. They remain in that directory until Trash is emptied, and can be recovered if they have not been dumped.

This is very similar to the Windows recycle bin, but one important difference is that files deleted from floppy discs are stored in Trash until it is emptied. With Windows a file on a floppy disc that is placed in the Recycle Bin is actually deleted from the disc and is not copied into the Recycle Bin. This makes it impossible to recover the file, except (possibly) with the aid of an undelete program. KDE is more accommodating, and the file is copied to trash where it can be copied back to the original disc, or to anywhere else.

The icons on the desktop simply provide immediate access to a certain point in the file system. If you login as "root" the Trash folder will be /root/Desktop/Trash. If you login as (say) "Fred", the Trash folder will be /home/Fred/Desktop/Trash. Deleted files are stored in this folder until the Trash is emptied, and until then they can be treated just like any other files. Of course, files in Trash are still on the hard disc, and take up space on the disc until the Trash is emptied. In fact deleting files on floppy discs by putting them into the Trash folder adds more files to the hard disc and reduces the amount of free storage space.

Autostart

The "Autostart" icon provides access to a folder that contains programs or links to programs that must be run when KDE starts up. This is the equivalent of the autoexec.bat file in MS/DOS and the Startup folder in Windows 95/98. Each user has their own Autostart folder, and can have their own choice of programs (if any) operating when KDE starts. In fact each user effectively has his or her own KDE desktop which can be customised to suit individual requirements.

Templates

The Templates folder is, as you might have guessed, for storing template files. Do not concern yourself with this one for the time being. Many programs can use templates to save time when producing standard letters, book layouts, drawings, or whatever. Should you start using templates they can be stored in this folder.

The Panel

The Panel is the bar across the bottom of the screen, and in Windows terminology this is a form of toolbar, but it has similarities with the Windows Taskbar. The KDE 1.0 Panel looks rather more busy than the 1.1 version. With both versions there are icons that provide a quick means to run certain programs, but by default KDE 1.1 has rather fewer of these icons. Both versions have four "buttons" labelled "one" to "four". These are used to switch between the KDE equivalent of virtual consoles, but they are virtual desktops. When using the graphical user interface Linux can undertake multi-tasking, but there are two ways of tackling this. You can simply run two or more programs on one desktop, much as you would with a Windows system, or you can have a separate desktop for each program. In fact you can use both methods, with several programs running on each virtual desktop.

If it will be necessary to have access to two programs at once, such as when dragging and dropping a file from one window to another, it is obviously necessary to have both windows open at once. They must then be open on the same desktop. If two large and separate programs are being run, and there is no need for any dragging and dropping, then it is probably best if they are run full-screen on separate desktops. You could have something like a word processor, a graphics program, a spreadsheet, and a database running on separate virtual desktops, with instant switching from one to the other via the Panel. Bear in mind though, that the more programs that are multi-tasked, the greater the system resources that will be needed. For complex multi-tasking to work well it is essential to have plenty of memory available. With the current low cost of PC memory this is not normally a major problem.

To the left of the buttons used to switch between virtual consoles there are two much smaller buttons. The upper one can be used to logout of the KDE session. This takes the system back into a console mode and the command line interpreter. On operating this button you get a chance to change your mind (in case you operated it by accident) or to continue with the logout. If you are using the "root" account you may be given further options such as shutting down the system, exiting to a console, or rebooting. The lower of the two small buttons is the screen-locking button.

Now you see it...

You will notice that the Panel has an arrow at each end. If you try left clicking on the right-hand arrow you will find that the Panel appears to retract into the right-hand side of the screen. Similarly, left clicking on the left-hand button causes the panel to retract into the left-hand side of the screen. In either case the arrow remains on the screen, and clicking on it again causes the Panel to pop back out again. When the Panel is displayed on the screen a full-screen window will occupy the area above the Panel, but will not

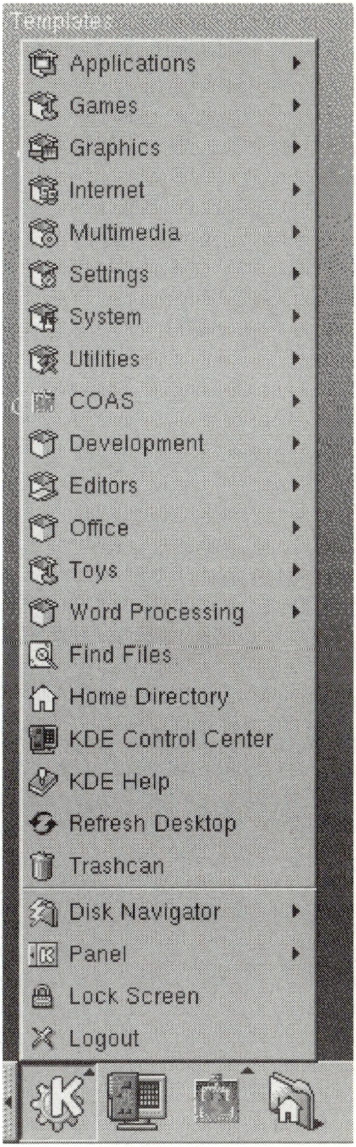

Fig.3.2 The "K" popup menu

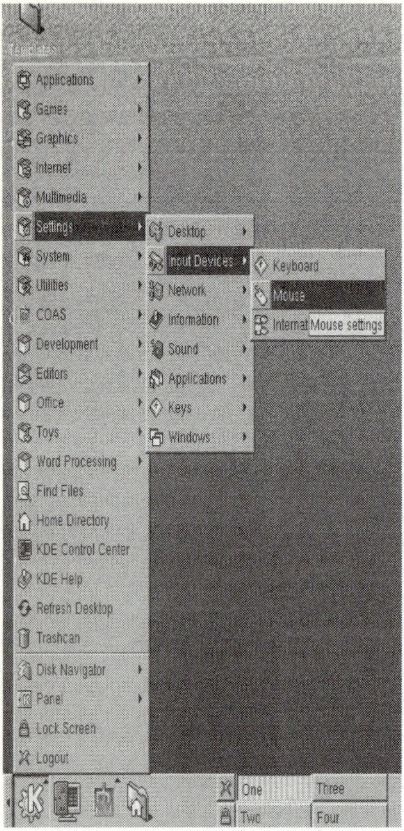

Fig.3.3 There are numerous programs available via submenus

cover it. To use a genuine full-screen window the Panel must be retracted and the window maximised. This is rather like hiding the Taskbar in Windows, and it can be automatically hidden if desired.

Programs

The button at the left-hand end of the Taskbar marked with a large letter "K" produces a pop-up menu if you left click on it (Figure 3.2). This button is very similar to the Windows Start button, and the menu system provides access to various programs, the on-line help system, control panels, a means of logging out, etc. Some of the menu items have fly-outs that provide further menu options, and some of the fly-outs have further fly-outs (Figure 3.3). When initially experimenting with KDE it is worthwhile trying out some of these programs and the help system as this is a good way to familiarise yourself with the way the KDE desktop is used. The Mahjongg and Asteroids games, plus the Gimp and *xv* graphics programs are well worth a try. To run a program you simply left click on the appropriate menu item.

Taskbar

The Taskbar is at the top of the screen, and like its Windows equivalent it shows all windows that are currently running, even if they have been minimised and are only running in the background. When you minimise

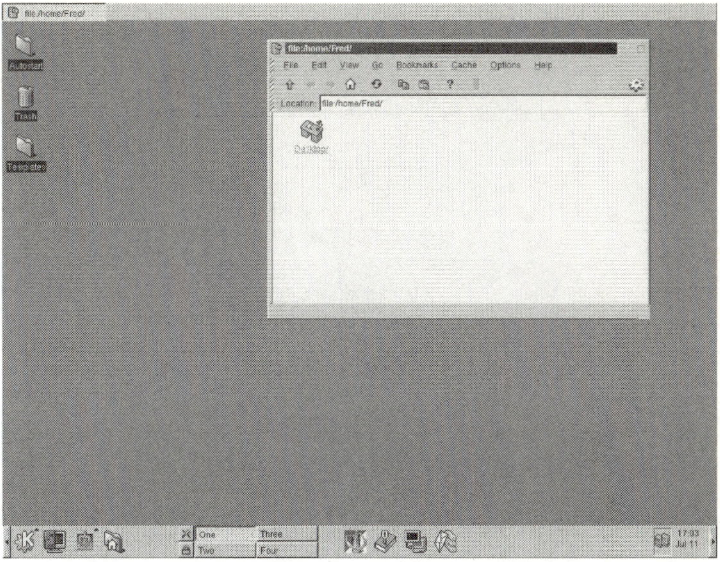

Fig.3.4 KFM window is normally open when KDE is first run

a Window it folds up and moves into its section of the Taskbar. To reactivate the window you simply left click on its section of the Taskbar. This is all the KDE Taskbar does, and it is rather more limited in scope than the Windows equivalent. The Panel and Taskbar together are roughly equivalent to the Windows Taskbar.

KFM

There may be a window open when KDE starts up (Figure 3.4). This is normally present by default, and the program running in the window is KFM. This program is central to using KDE, and it is essential to spend some time familiarising yourself with the way it operates. KFM is the KDE file manager program, and its equivalent in Windows 95/98 is Windows Explorer. Using KFM you can browse the Linux file system, run programs, copy, delete and rename files, and much else besides. In other words, you use KFM to do many of the general file management tasks that would otherwise be handled using the command line interpreter. If KFM is not running, left click on the house-like icon in the Panel. This will run a copy of KFM that starts in the home directory (e.g. /root if you login as “root”).

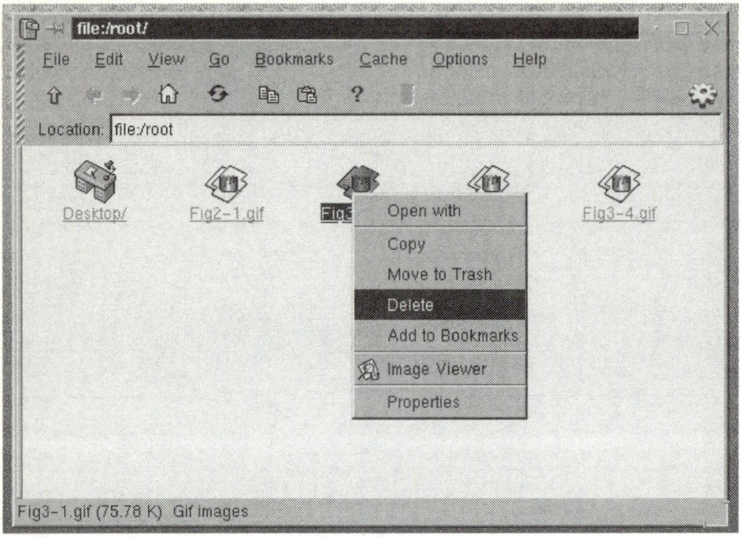

Fig.3.5 Right clicking on an icon brings up this menu

Using KFM is not quite the same as using Windows Explorer, but there are strong similarities. Figure 3.5 shows a close-up view of a KFM window. The main area at the bottom of the KFM window shows the files and folders in the current folder. These are displayed as icons with the relevant name shown below the icon. If there are too many icons to fit into the window a scrollbar will be displayed at the right-hand side of the window. The contents of the window can then be scrolled up and down by dragging the button in the scrollbar. Alternatively, the window can be scrolled by a large amount by clicking just above or below the button, or in small increments by clicking on the arrowheads at the ends of the bar. The KDE scrollbars would seem to work in identical fashion to their Windows counterparts.

Opening folders

There are different icons for the various file categories and for folders, and they are mostly easy to fathom. For example, a representation of a cardboard folder is used for normal folders, and a gearwheel icon represents program files. To examine the contents of a folder you simply left click on it, and the main screen area changes to show its contents. Note that a single click is all that is required, not double-clicking as in

Windows. In fact a lot of double clicking in Windows is replaced by single clicks in Linux, but some double clicking is still required. This is likely to cause a few errors at first, and you may find that you keep opening two copies of a program instead of one.

Brief details of a file or folder are provided in the status line at the bottom of the window if you place the cursor over an icon. With appropriate file types you can left click on the icons to open the files. As in Windows, this approach to things is dependent on the operating system having a program registered to deal with the type of file you select. There should be no problem with the standard file types, such as PDF, GIF, JPG, and plain text files. Right clicking on an icon brings up a small menu, as in Figure 3.5. This menu gives access to some basic tasks.

Delete/Trash

The delete option is effectively the same as using the *rm* command of the command line interpreter. A file deleted in this fashion is not copied to Trash, and has to be regarded as lost and gone forever. Copying to Trash is the same as dragging the file to the Trash icon, and it can be recovered until it is emptied from Trash.

Open with

This option brings up a dialogue box into which the name of the program (including the path) used to open the file is typed. Alternatively, the Browse option can be used to locate and launch the file (Figure 3.6). Note that it in this case is necessary to double left click on a folder or program in order to open it.

Copy

This is very much like copying to the Windows Clipboard. Having copied the file, you can then move to another folder and right click anywhere in the main window area. This brings up a menu that includes a Paste option. Selecting this copies the file into the current folder. The KFM copy/paste facility is much like the Windows equivalent, but there is no cut/paste feature. It is not even available in the form of a move facility in this menu. The file must be copied to its new destination with the original then being deleted, or the file must be dragged to its new destination with the Move option then being selected.

Image viewer

If the file is a recognised graphics type there will be the option of viewing it using the KDE image viewer program.

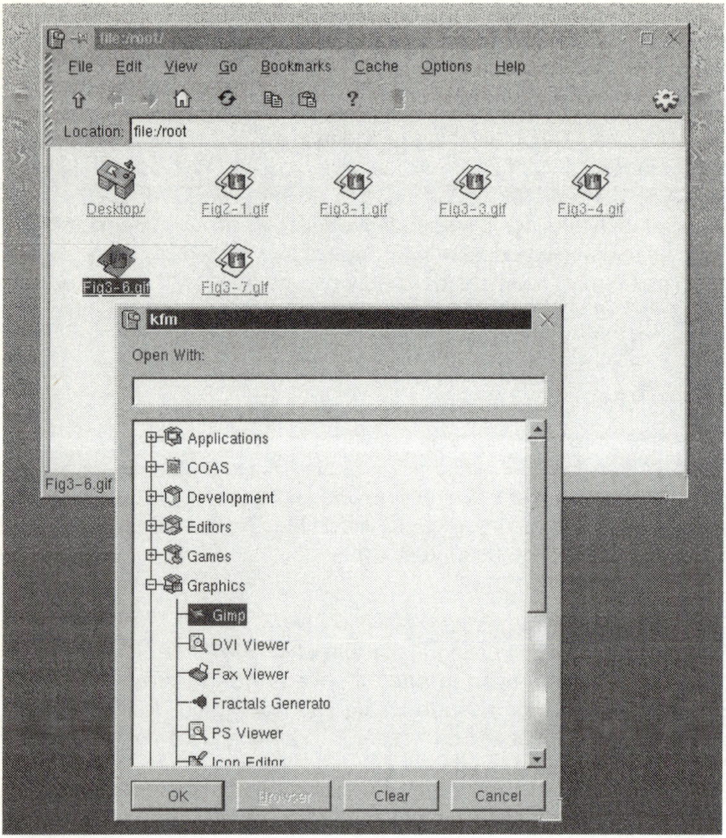

Fig.3.6 The Open With browser option

Text editor

If the file is a text type it can be loaded into a text editor program using this option.

Add to Bookmarks

The Linux file system tends to be rather complex, and many files are buried away quite deep in it. The Bookmarks facility is extremely useful, and provides a quick means of accessing files that will be used quite often, but are deep in the file system. Selecting this option adds the file

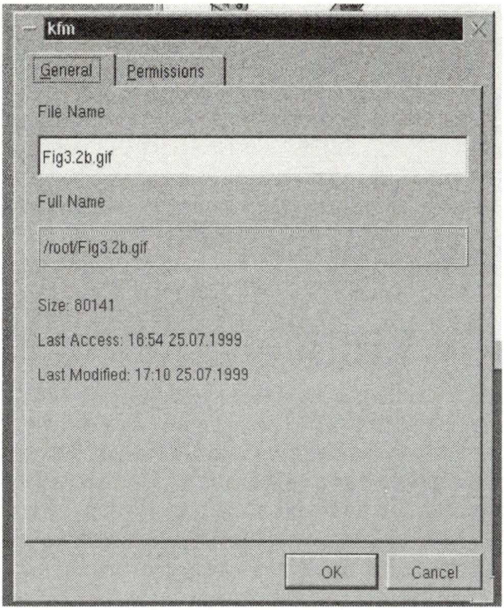

Fig.3.7 The Proprties dialogue box can be used to rename a file

to the Bookmarks list. To access the file via its Bookmark activate the Bookmarks menu and then select the file from the list.

Properties

The Properties option brings up a screen (Figure 3.7) that shows some basic information on the file. The name of the file is shown in an editable text box, and by altering this text the name of the file can be altered. Of course, this is not possible if the file is a read-only type, such as a file on a CD-ROM. Left clicking on the Permissions tab brings up an alternative screen, which gives information on the read and write status of the file, its owner and group information.

Navigation

There is an edit box immediately above the main window area, and this shows the current path. You can type in a path here in order to go direct to a specific directory. Just enter the path and press Return. Typing the path and a file or program name and then pressing the Return key opens the file or program.

Above the edit box is the navigation toolbar. This provides a quick and easy way of moving around the file system. The three arrows that point up, left, and right respectively move up one level, backwards one step, and forwards one step. Obviously it is not possible to move one step backwards until you have moved from the original directory, or to move one step forward until you have moved backwards. Also, it is not possible to move further up the directory tree once the system is in the root (/) directory. Any arrow buttons that are inoperative appear to be recessed into the toolbar, whereas buttons that can be used appear to protrude slightly from the bar. The next button in this toolbar has a house-like icon, and this moves KFM straight to the home directory.

Reload

The button having a circle icon with two arrows is the Reload button. When copying and moving files, or perhaps when changing discs, you may sometimes find that the icons in the main window area do not seem to properly reflect the contents of the directory. Operating the Reload button will update the window, and it should then provide an accurate account of the directory's contents.

Copy and paste

The next two buttons respectively provide access to the copy and paste facilities. Before you can copy something it must be selected in the main window area. In Windows an object is selected by left clicking on it, but with KFM this will open it. Instead, point just outside the icon area, hold down the left mouse button, and then drag a frame line around the icon or icons you wish to select. The selected icons will change to dark blue in colour. Another way of selecting multiple files is to hold down the Control key and then left click on each file that you wish to select. This is the method that must be used if you wish to select files that are not conveniently grouped together on the screen. It is, of course, the same method that is used to select a group of files in Windows. Once selected the files can be copied using the copy button. Groups of files can also be dragged to another KFM window, dragged to Trash, etc., and can generally be treated as a single entity.

Help

The next button is the help button, and pressing this activates the KFM on-line help system). KDE help systems work in much the same way as their Windows equivalents. Left clicking on an underlined word moves the system into a page dealing with that topic. The larger help programs include the usual search facilities. Help systems in general have a reputation for stating the obvious and offering little of real substance, but there is some useful advice to be found if you delve into the KDE help systems.

Stop

The final button is, in theory at any rate, the stop button. In most cases the program will operate so quickly that it is literally a case of "if you blink you miss it". However, it can take many seconds to deal with directories that contain huge numbers of files, and by pressing the stop button things can be brought to a halt.

In Control

At the top of the KFM screen there is a title bar. This bar is present on all X Windows programs, and it does more than spell out the name of the program. There are a number of control buttons here, but not all of these buttons are present on every program window. The button at the right-hand end of the bar marked with a cross, like its Windows equivalent, is used to close the window. The button next to it that is marked with a square is again much like the Windows Maximise button found in the same place, but with a slightly different marking. Left-clicking on this button causes the window to run in full-screen mode, and clicking on it again returns the window to its normal size. The next button to the right is marked with a dot and is the Iconify button. It is equivalent to the Windows Minimise button. Right-clicking on this button causes the window to disappear into the taskbar. Clicking on the appropriate section of the taskbar restores the window. Anyone used to using Windows should find these buttons easy to use, as they are essentially the same as their Windows counterparts.

Window button

The button at the left-hand end of the title bar is the window button, and operating this activates a pop-down menu (Figure 3.8). The Maximise, Iconify, and Close options simply duplicate the three buttons described previously. Resize, unsurprisingly, enables the size of the window to be altered. Selecting this option produces a frame that can be dragged to the required size using the mouse, and left clicking the mouse then causes the window to change to the selected size. This is really a duplicate function as well, since any window can be dragged to the required size. Placing the cursor at the edge or corner of a window causes the cursor to change shape. The window can then be resized by holding down the left mouse button, dragging it to the required size, and then releasing the button. This is again standard Windows style control. A window can be dragged around the screen by pointing to the title section of the title bar, holding down the left mouse button, and then

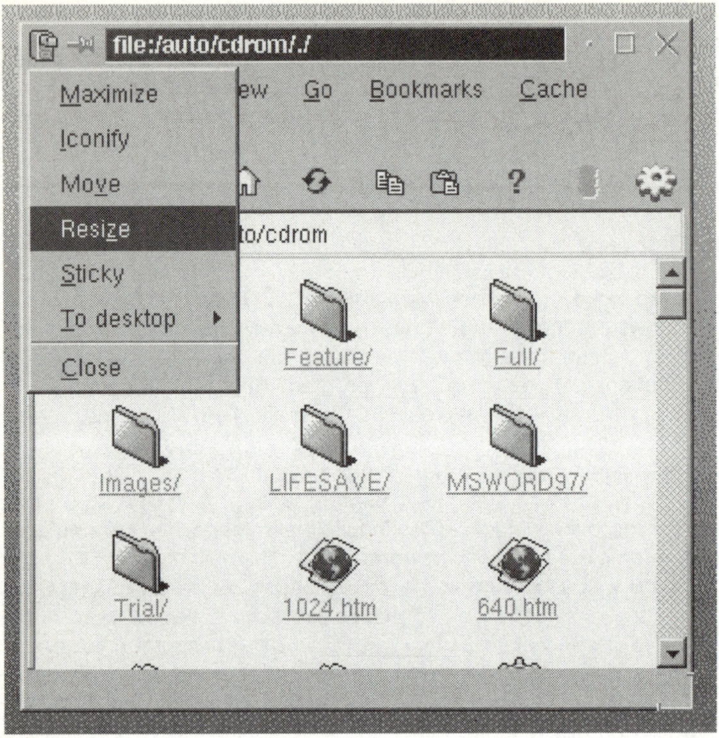

Fig.3.8 The window button popdown menu

moving the cursor. The window will move with the cursor until the left button is released.

It is possible to move a window so that the title bar disappears "under" the Taskbar, which on the face of it leaves no way of dragging the window back down the screen. This is in fact possible, and it is just a matter of pressing the Alt key and then dragging the window into the desired position. Having pressed the Alt key it is possible to drag the window using any part of it as a handle.

Stick button

The button next to the window button is the Stick or Pin button. Its icon is meant to represent a pin. Windows are not normally "pinned" in place on the screen, and disappear from the screen when switching from one virtual desktop to another. Left clicking on the stick button fixes the window on the screen so that it remains in place when changing from one virtual desktop to another. Clicking on this button again releases the window. The icon changes when it is activated, and it shows a view looking down onto the head of the pin when the window is "pinned" in place, and the pin set horizontally when it is not. You can simply stick a window in place so that it is available using all the virtual desktops, or move it from one desktop to another by sticking it in place, changing desktops, and then releasing it again. Windows does not have virtual desktops, and consequently has no equivalent to this feature.

Menu bar

Beneath the title bar KFM has the usual menu bar. There are numerous options available via these menus, and we will only consider some of the more useful ones here. To add a new folder off the current directory, activate the File menu and then select New and Folder (Figure 3.9). Type the name for the new folder in the dialogue box that then appears, left-click on OK, and the icon for the newly created folder will appear in the main screen area. The New Window option runs another copy of KFM, which starts in the current directory, but you can move on to other directories if necessary.

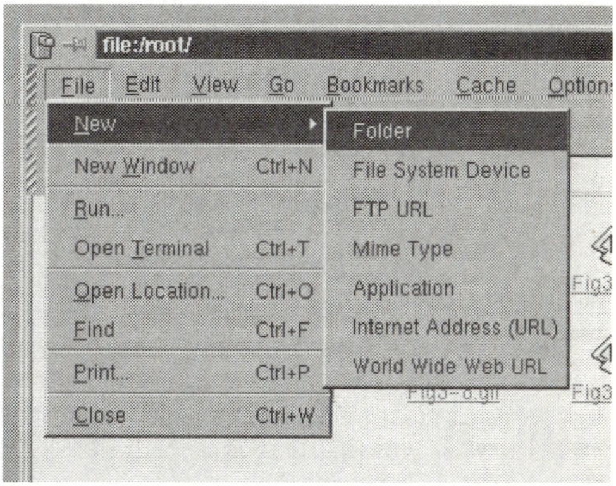

Fig.3.9 Adding a new folder via the Edit menu

This is useful when moving or copying files. The copy and paste method described earlier can be used, but it is often easier to have two copies of KFM open and to simply drag files from one window to another. Once a file has been dragged across and released a three-option menu will appear. This enables the file to be copied, moved, or linked. Note that with this method of copying it is possible to copy the file and delete the original in one go. Simply select the Move option. It also provides an easy means of

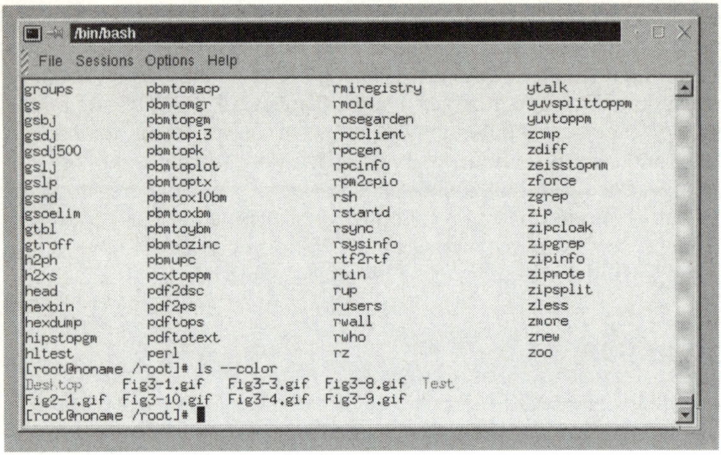

Fig.3.10 A terminal (console) running in a KDE window

generating links. Try generating a link and look at the filename that appears beneath its icon. This is in italics to indicate that it is only a link and not the "real thing".

Program icons

Note that file icons can be dragged from a window onto the desktop. With Windows it is common practice to have a desktop practically filled with program icons, and in order to run a program it is merely necessary to double click on its icon. With Linux it is possible to have the same sort of set-up, and it is just a matter of dragging each program icon onto the KDE desktop selecting the link option. In order to run a program it is then just a matter of left clicking on its desktop icon. Do not double click on the icon or you will run two copies of the program!

KDE console

The Open Terminal option of the File menu runs a console in a KDE window (Figure 3.10). This console can be used much like an ordinary bash shell, with commands being typed in. You can even use the — color option with the ls command. You will notice that keyboard shortcuts are given for some of the options on the menus. For example, Control-t launches a console when KFM is running. As always, you need to be careful when using multiple windows and keyboard shortcuts, because the shortcuts only provide the desired result if the right window is active at the time.

View window

The Edit menu duplicates the editing features (copy, delete, etc.) available by other means. The View menu (Figure 3.11) controls the way in which information is displayed in the main screen area, and offers some useful features. Files having names that start with a full stop are normally hidden and do not appear in the main window area. When the Show Hidden Files option is active, as indicated by a tick in the box next to it in the menu, these hidden files are shown normally. If you go to the /root directory and switch on this option you should find a large increase in the number of files displayed.

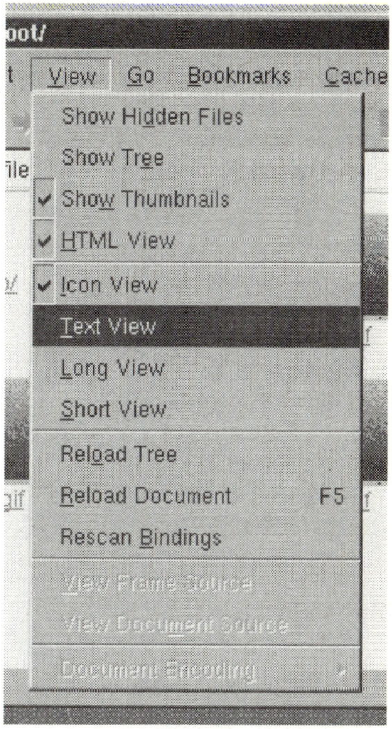

Fig.3.11 The KFM Edit menu

Thumbnail view

Activating the Show Thumbnails option results in the icons for most types of graphic file being displayed as miniature versions of the picture contained in the files (Figure 3.12). This makes it easy to select the required file, but with a large number of graphics files in a directory it can take a while for them all to be displayed.

Show Tree

The tree view (Figure 3.13) splits the main screen area and adds a directory tree to the left-hand side of the main window area. This shows three folders initially, which are the root (/), My Home, and Desktop folders. To open a folder click on the small triangular shaped button beside it. The triangle then points downward to show that the folder is

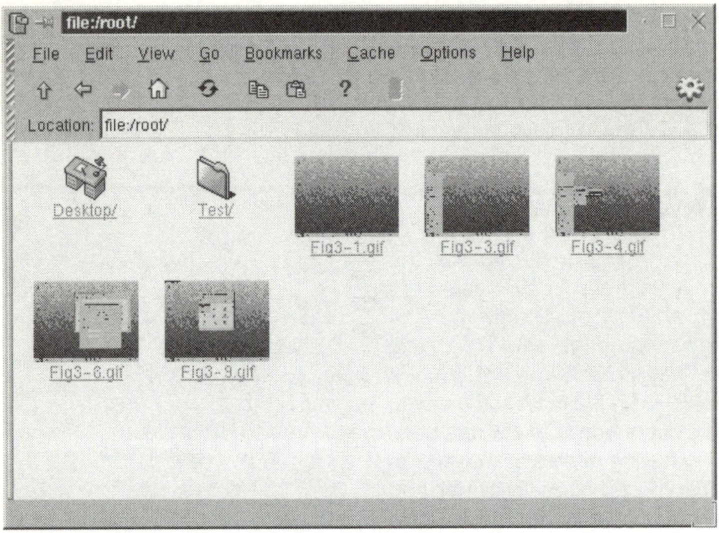

Fig.3.12 KFM with the Thumbnail option selected

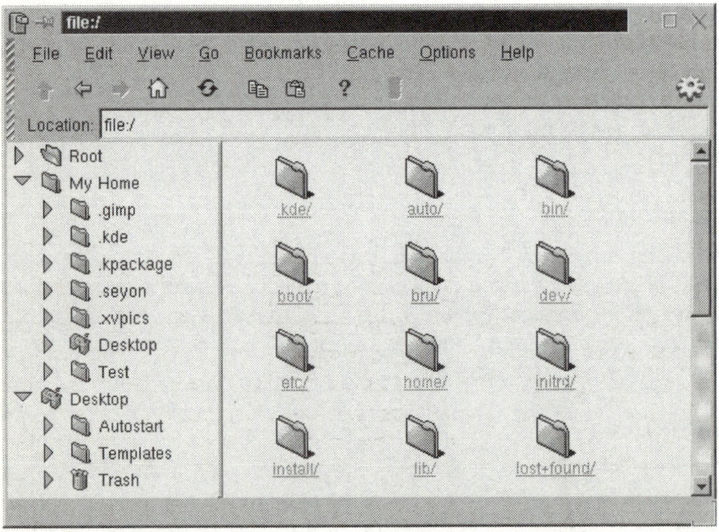

Fig.3.13 The left section of the screen shows a Tree View

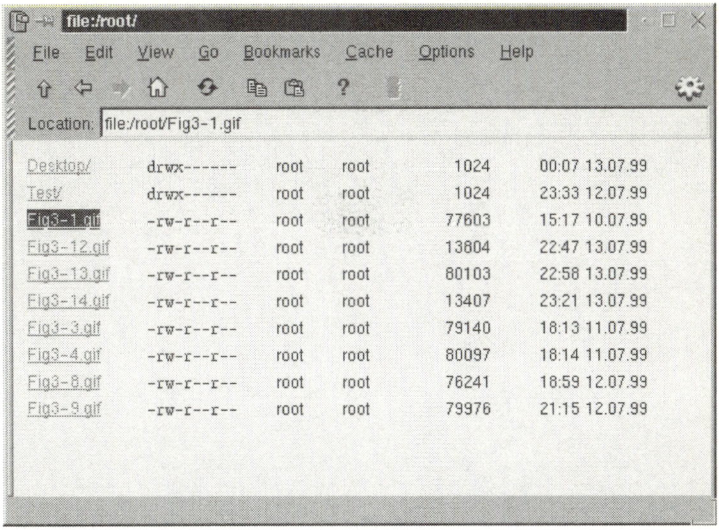

Fig.3.14 The KFM Text View offers an alternative to icons

open and its contents will then be shown beneath it. Note that in this context the contents of a folder are other folders, and not files. Opening a folder in the tree view does not result in any change to the files shown in the right-hand section of the main screen area. The tree view is simply there to help you navigate around a complex directory structure, and is really just a map of the directory structure.

Text view

When using the text view the icons disappear and are replaced by lines of text giving the name and brief details of each file or directory (Figure 3.14). This can be a better way of handling things if a directory contains a large number of files. Using the icons can result in what is effectively a few metres of window to scroll through! You can open a file or folder by left clicking on its filename, but not on the information to the right of the filename. The filename can also be dragged to another window. Folder names are in magenta print, and filenames are in red print.

Short view

The short view option is a form of text display, but unlike the long view text mode it gives only the filename and no details (Figure 3.15). As in

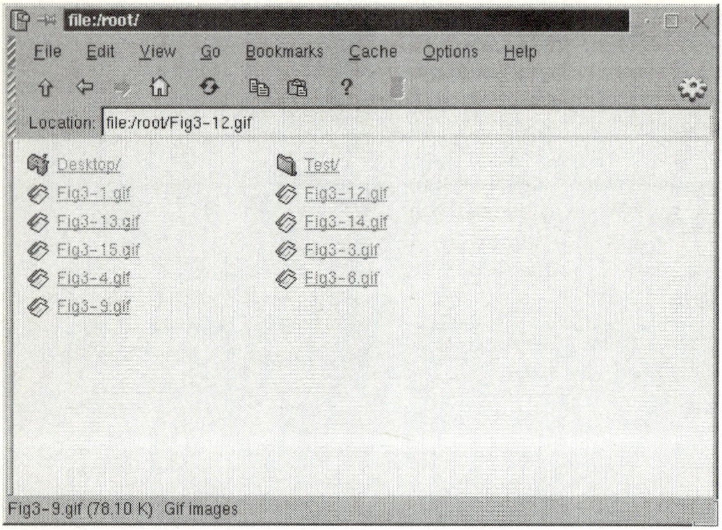

Fig.3.15 Files displayed using the KFM Short Text View

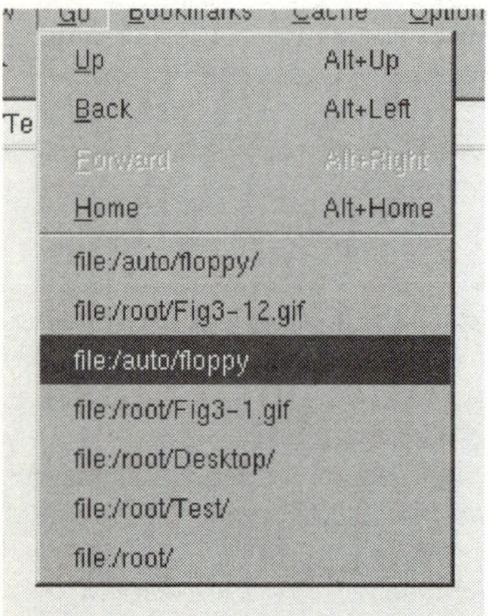

Fig.3.16 The KFM history palette

the icon mode, placing the cursor over a filename results in some brief details of the file being shown in the status line at the bottom of the window. For a directory containing a really large number of files this is the most practical mode to use.

Go

At the bottom of the Go menu you will find a list of files and folders that have recently been opened using KFM (Figure 3.16). This is much the same as a file history list in Windows and anything in the list can be opened by selecting it.

Options

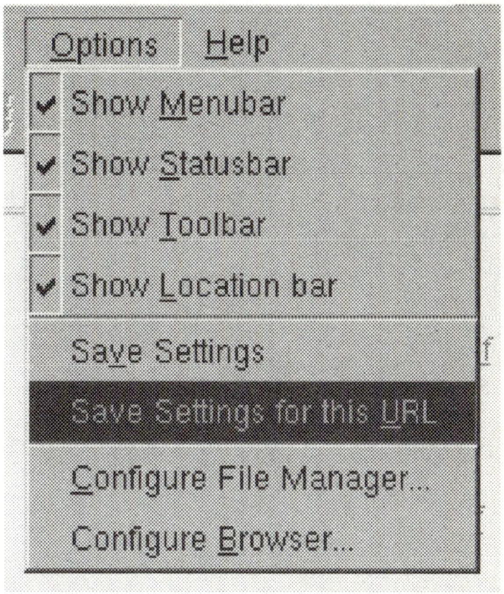

Fig.3.17 The KFM Option menu

The Options menu (Figure 3.17) enables the menu bar, status bar, location bar, and toolbar to be switched on and off, as required. Using the Save Settings option saves the current settings as the defaults, and they will be used whenever KFM is run in the future. Of course, these defaults are different for each user, and other users' settings are not affected when this option is used. The Configure File Manager option brings up another menu (Figure 3.18) which enables things such as the text font and colour to be changed. If you are using high resolution with a relatively small monitor it is a good idea to increase the font size from the default setting of

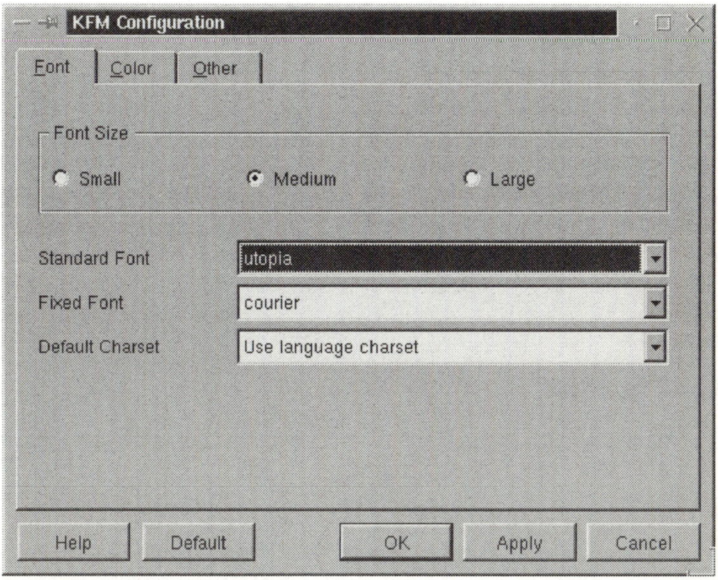

Fig.3.18 The KFM configuration menu

"small" to "medium" or even "large". This makes the labels under icons and the lists of files in text view modes much easier to read.

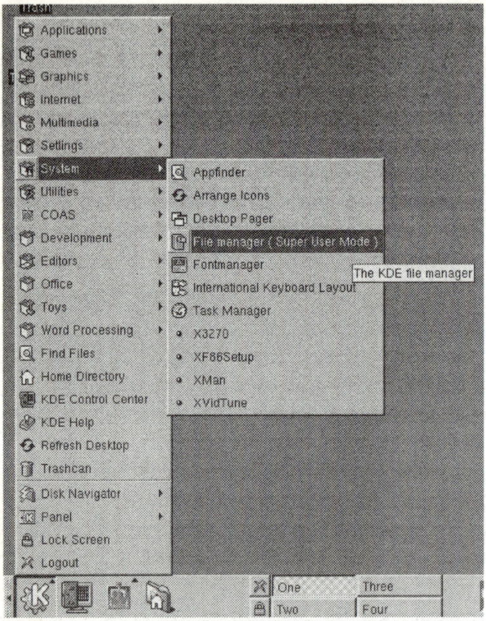

Fig.3.19 Starting KFM in the superuser mode

In the red

If you login as "root", each KFM window will have a red bar just to the left of the word "file" in the menu bar. This is a reminder that you have supervisor or superuser status, and can make changes to system files that could mess up the system. In this mode it is necessary to exercise more caution than normal, especially when experimenting with KFM. If you login as something other than "root" it is still possible to run KFM in the super-user mode. Left click on the "K" button on the panel, and then select System from the menu. From the fly-out menu (Figure 3.19) choose the File Manager (Super User Mode) option. This will open a console where you will be asked for the password. Enter the "root" password and a copy of KFM with superuser privileges (and the red "flag") will then open.

KFM and tar files

KFM makes it easy to examine the contents of tar files and even zipped tar files. These have "tar", "tgz", and "gz" file extensions. If you left click on the icon for a file of this type the effect is very much like opening a folder. The KFM main window changes to show the contents of the file, as in the example shown in Figure 3.20. With a text file such as a readme file you can often view its contents by left clicking on the icon. Figure 3.21 shows the contents of a Corel WordPerfect readme file displayed in

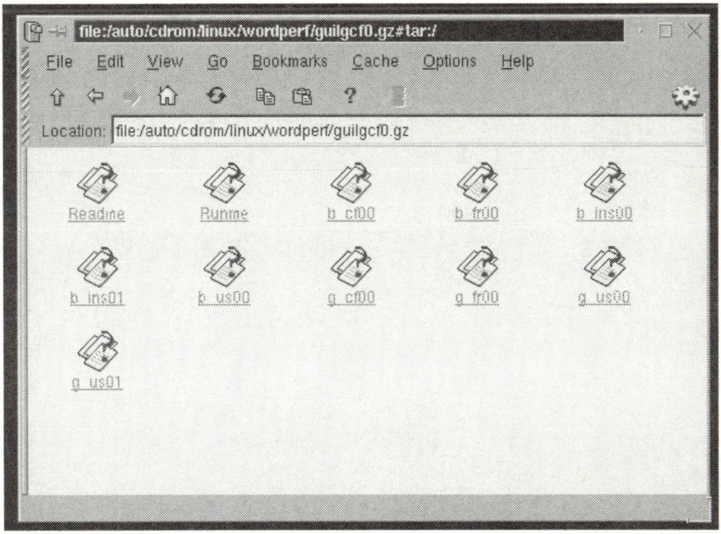

Fig.3.20 KFM displaying the contents of an archive file

a Kedit window using this method. It is often possible to view graphics files in the same way, provided they are in a format that can be handled by Kview. Files within a tar archive can be copied and possibly even deleted by using the same methods that are used for ordinary files. What can be achieved seems to depend on the files in question and the version of KDE you are using, so it is necessary to use the "suck it and see" method to determine what can and can not be achieved. One slight problem when dealing with files in an archive is that more processing is required to deal with files in this form. The practical result is that things tend to run much more slowly than normal, but this is a small price to pay for the convenience of being able to manipulate the file so easily.

Floppy copy

Like the Linux command line, KDE does not have a built-in copy facility for floppy discs. It is not possible to make an exact clone of a floppy disc, but using KFM it is reasonably easy to copy all the data from a floppy disc to a blank disc. The obvious method is to place the original disc in the drive and left click on its icon, and then use Select All and copy from the Edit menu. With a change to the blank disc and a press

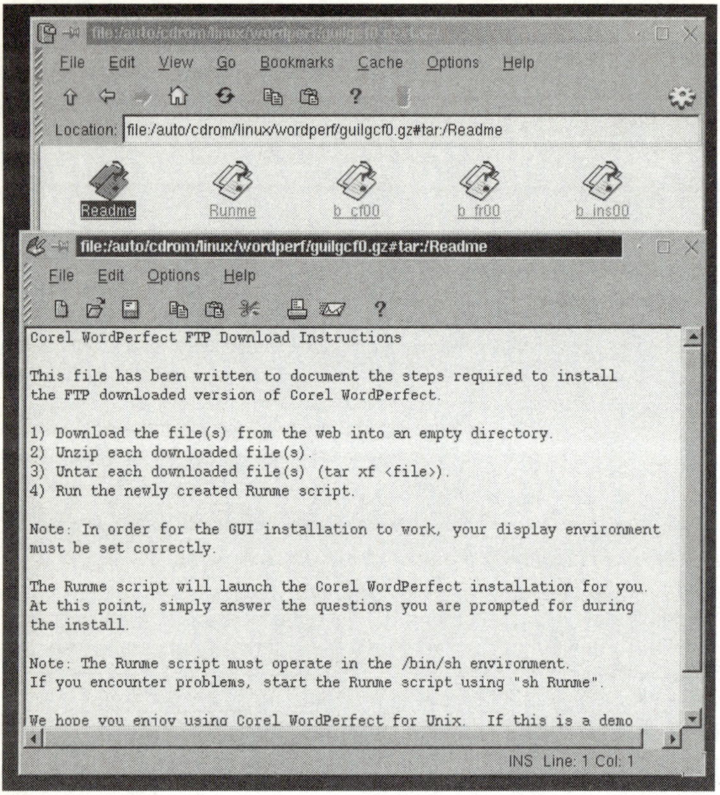

Fig.3.21 KFM displaying the text within an archived file

of the Reload button it should then be possible to paste the files onto the new disc. In fact this will not work, because without the original disc in the drive and accessible to the system there is no source for KFM to copy from.

To get around this it is necessary to use a longer route, which is the KFM equivalent to the command line method of copying described in chapter 2. Put the original floppy disc into the drive, left click on its icon, and then use Select all from the edit menu. Drag the files to an empty temporary directory opened in another copy of KFM and select Copy from the popup menu. If there are only a few files they can simply be dragged and copied onto the desktop. Replace the original disc with the copy disc, and operate the Reload button. Select all of the files in

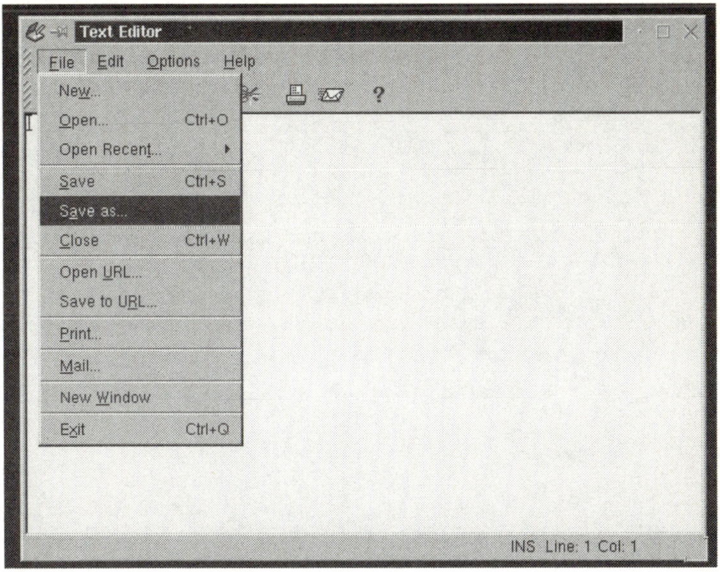

Fig.3.22 The standard version of the Kedit text editor

the temporary folder or on the desktop and drag them to the KFM window for the floppy disc. Select Move from the popup menu and wait while the files are copied to the floppy disc. The files in the temporary folder or on the desktop will be automatically deleted. If you use a temporary folder this will remain on the hard disc, but it is probably best to leave it there for possible future use.

Text editing

There are several text editors to choose from when using KDE. When you open a text file via KFM it is loaded into Kedit. There are actually two versions of this program available via the "K" menu system. The normal version is accessed via Applications and Text Editor (Figure 3.22). A slightly more advanced version of the program is available via Applications and then Advanced Editor (Figure 3.23). Both versions are similar to the Wordpad program that is normally installed with Windows 95 and 98, but they lack some of the text formatting facilities. These programs are really designed to act as text editors rather than mini word processors. As such, they lack one or two features of Wordpad. On the

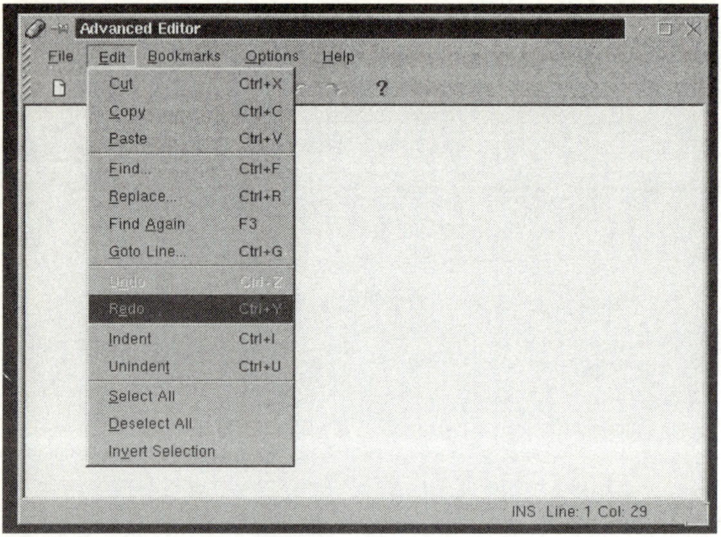

Fig.3.23 The deluxe version of Kedit has a few more menu options

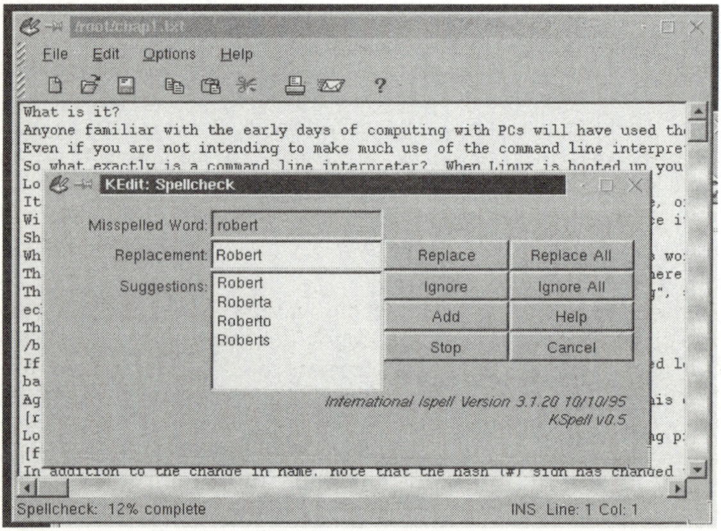

Fig.3.24 Kedit has some advanced features including a spelling checker

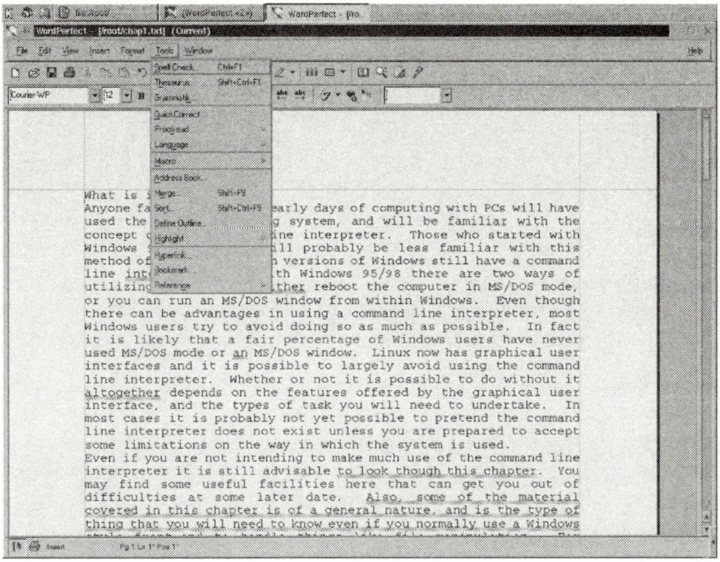

Fig.3.25 WordPerfect for Linux is a full-feature word processor

other hand, there are some quite advanced facilities, such as a built-in spelling checker (Figure 3.24). Both versions also have a useful Find facility.

WordPerfect

Many versions of Linux are now supplied with so-called "personal" editions of commercial software. The exact conditions of use vary, but this type of software is normally complete and can be used for non-commercial purposes. Naturally enough, support for free software such as this is either very limited or non-existent, as are printed manuals. If your version of Linux is supplied complete with Corel WordPerfect 8 (Figure 3.25) it is certainly worthwhile installing this. If you have insufficient hard disc space to accommodate the program, buy a bigger disc! WordPerfect is one of the most advanced word processors available, and it is suitable for everything from a quick letter to a "War and Peace" size novel or a complex technical manual. I have used various versions WordPerfect to write dozens of books.

The Linux version is not an exact clone of the Windows program, but it is very close. If you have used WordPerfect for Windows, or any other Windows word processor for that matter, using WordPerfect 8 for Linux should not present any major difficulties. It has an advanced spelling checker, thesaurus, grammar checker, the ability to insert graphics into documents and all the other features you would expect from an up-market word processor. One slight quirk is that multiple documents are opened by running multiple copies of WordPerfect, but you can still cut/copy and paste from one document to another.

Last and by no means least, there is XEmacs, the X Windows version of the *emacs* word processor (Figure 3.26). If you are unable to find it in the menu system it will probably be possible to run it by entering this command into a KDE terminal:

xemacs

In fact you will probably be greeted with XEmacs if you try to run the standard version of the program from a KDE terminal. This program would seem to have all the power of the standard version, but its menu system and toolbar make it much easier for newcomers to master.

Recap

After reading through the above material and experimenting with KFM you should soon be able to navigate your way around the system and undertake simple basic "housekeeping" tasks such as copying and deleting files. Here is a quick recapitulation of how some of the more common tasks are performed. Note that in most cases there is actually more than one way of performing the task, and that not all the possible methods are necessarily included here.

Drag with the mouse

Point to the scrollbar (or whatever), hold down the left mouse button, move the mouse to make the required adjustment, and then release the left mouse button.

Selecting files

Hold down the Control key and left click on the file or files you wish to select. Alternatively, hold down the left mouse button and drag a frame around the file or files. You can also select files using the frame method,

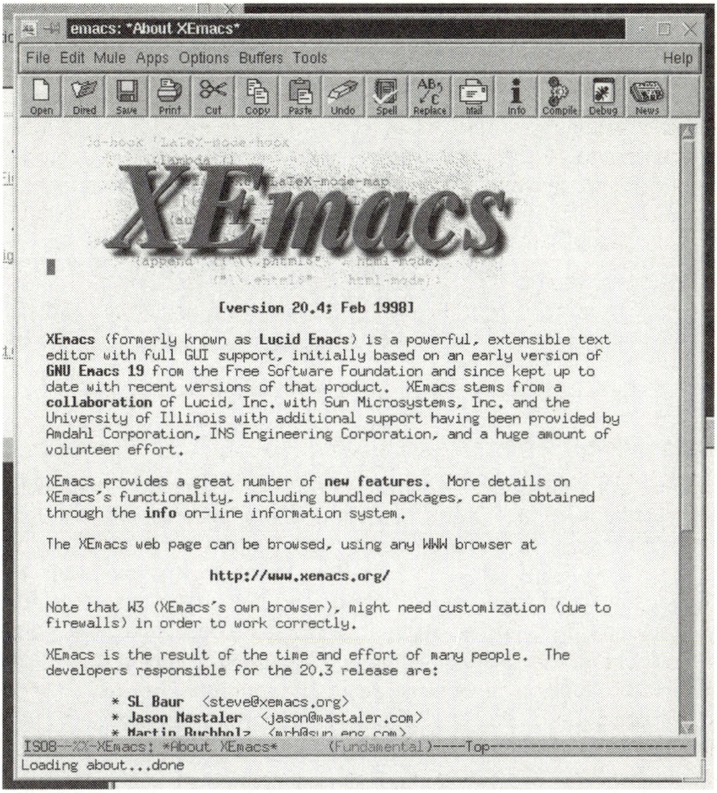

Fig.3.26 The XEmacs editor has a menu system and a toolbar

and then add additional files to the selection by holding down the Control key and left clicking on the appropriate icons. You can not hold down the Control key and add to a selection using the frame method.

Select all files in a folder

Open the folder and then choose Select All from the Edit menu.

Open a file or folder

Locate it using KFM and then left click on its icon or filename. If the file is not a program or a standard data type you will then have to select the program needed to open the file.

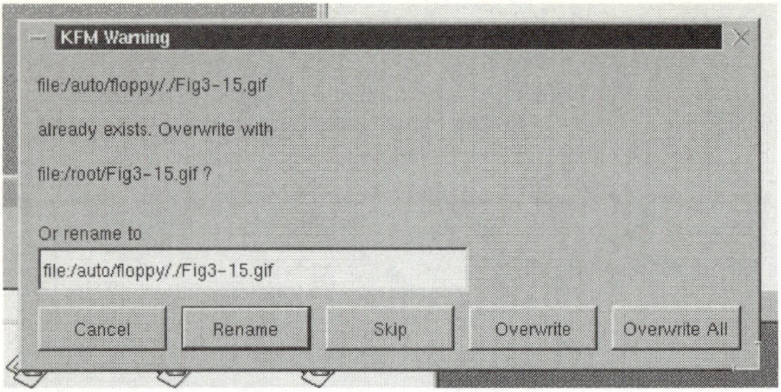

Fig.3.27 KFM will not overwrite a file unless told to do so

Copy, Move, Link

Open two copies of KFM, one showing the source folder and one showing the destination folder. Select the item or items to be copied and drag them to a vacant screen area in the main window for the destination folder. Select Copy, Move or Link from the menu that pops up, as required. An alternative method of copying is to select the items and then choose Copy from the Edit menu. Open the destination folder and then select Paste from the edit menu. If a folder is copied or moved, so are all its contents.

Overwriting

If you try to copy a file to a folder that already contains a file having the same name, KFM will produce the pop-up menu of Figure 3.27. If you left click on the Overwrite button the source file will replace the destination file. This enables a new version of a file to be inserted in place of an old version. It can also result in an old file obliterating a new one if you are not careful! When dealing with groups of files, Overwrite All will result in any files having duplicate names being overwritten. This obviously requires even more care to be exercised.

Trash and Delete

Select the items to be moved into Trash and drag them to the Trash icon. To delete items select them and then choose Delete from the Edit menu. Alternatively, select one or more items and then right click on one of them. Select Delete from the pop-up menu. Note that deleted items can not be recovered.

Retrieving From Trash

Click on Trash to open its folder. The contents are then shown in a KFM window from where they can be copied and moved in the normal way.

Emptying Trash

Right click on Trash and then select Empty Trash Bin from the pop-up menu (Figure 3.28).

Fig.3.28 Emptying the Trash Bin

Close a window

Left click on the close button (the one marked with an "X") on the title bar. Alternatively, if the Close button is absent choose Close from the File menu. Using Control-w will close the active window.

Make a window active

Left click on an inactive part of the window, such as a part of the title bar that does not have any buttons. If you click on a button you will probably make the window active and operate the button as well. Only one window at a time can be active incidentally.

Move a window

Point to a part of the title bar that does not contain any buttons and then drag the window to the desired position. Alternatively, press the Alt key and then drag the window using any point within the window as a handle.

Minimise a window

Operate the Iconify button on the title bar (the button with a dot in the middle).

Restore a window

Left click on the appropriate section of the taskbar.

Maximise a window

Left click on its Maximise/Restore button (the button marked with a square). Clicking on it again takes the window back to its normal size.

Open a terminal (console)

Use Control-t from the keyboard, or operate the terminal button in the Panel (the one with the monitor icon).

Run a program

If it is not in the "K" menu, locate the program file using KFM and then left click on its icon or filename.

Put a program icon on the desktop

Locate the program file using KFM, and drag it onto a vacant area of the desktop. Select Link from the pop-up menu. Left clicking on the icon will then run the program.

Change virtual desktops

To move to another desktop simply left click on the appropriate desktop button on the panel (the buttons labelled from one to four). Alternatively, hold down the Control key and then keep pressing the Tab key to cycle through to the desktop you require.

Make a window visible in all desktops

Click on the Stick or Pin button in the title bar. Operating this button again makes the window visible only when using that particular desktop. This enables a window to be moved from one virtual desktop to another.

Start KFM

Click on the house icon in the panel. This starts a KFM in the Home directory, but you can move to the required directory from there.

Make a new folder

Open the parent directory using KFM. Right click on a vacant area of the main window, select New from the popup menu, and then Folder. Type the name of the new folder in the edit box that appears and then left click on OK.

Hide the Panel

Left click on an arrow at one end of the Panel. Left clicking on this arrow again restores the Panel.

Autostart a program

Locate the program file using KFM and then drag it to the Autostart icon. Then select Link from the pop-up menu.

Stop a program from starting automatically

To reverse the process left click on the Autostart icon. This opens a copy of KFM showing the contents of the Autostart folder. Simply delete the links for any programs that you do not require at start-up.

Make a window visible in all desktops

Activate its Sticky icon.

Move a window from one desktop to another

Activate its Sticky icon, switch to the desktop where it is required, and then deactivate the Sticky icon.

Note that some menu options and certain buttons are not operational under all circumstances. Inappropriate menu options are greyed-out (shown in light grey rather than black) and can not be selected. Similarly, inactive buttons do not appear to protrude slightly from the desktop, and can not be operated. This is the same method that is used in Windows and most other graphical user interfaces.

4

Also need to know

Multi-user

The three previous chapters covered the things you need to know in order to get Linux installed on your PC, and to use the system to run applications, copy files, etc., using either the command line interpreter or KDE. In this chapter we will delve a little deeper, covering a range of topics that you need to know about in order to use a Linux system effectively.

As we saw in previous chapters, in order to use Linux it is necessary to login under a user name, and to give the corresponding password. This is not done to make the boot-up process take even longer than normal, and there is a reason for doing things this way. Linux is a true multi-user operating system. Obviously with any operating system it is possible to have several people take it in turns to use the computer. Provided each user does not require much time at the computer a large number of people can use the computer in this way. The problem with this approach to things is that there is a lack of privacy for the users. This is not just a matter of other users having access to what might be someone else's private information. With a free-for-all approach to things there is a real danger of one user accidentally altering or erasing data belonging to other users. In fact the system could gradually degrade into a complete shambles.

With a multi-user operating system such as Linux you login under a name and password so that the operating system always knows who is using the computer. It would be an exaggeration to say that the system looks completely different to each user, and that it is like each one having their own PC. However, to some extent the computer will be personalised for the current user. The differences are perhaps more obvious when running KDE than when using the command line interpreter. Even when working at the command line there is a clear difference after logging in. The command line prompt is preceded by some text that includes the login name. Also, the system is in a directory specific to that user. For example, the system will normally be in /root if you login as "root", or /home/Fred if you login in as "Fred". Apart from "root", each user has a personal directory that is a subdirectory of the /home directory.

If you go into KDE there are more obvious differences. The KFM program that runs automatically at start-up is in the appropriate directory for the person using the computer, but the differences go well beyond that. If you put up program icons for the software that you use frequently, these will obviously be present when you login to KDE. Less obviously, they will not be present on the KDE desktop of any other user unless they also add them. Although the Trash, Templates and Autostart icons are present by default on every KDE desktop, they represent different folders for each user. For instance, other users can not use their Trash folders to access anything you place in your Trash folder. The Trash folder has the path /home/name/Desktop/Trash, where "name" is the login name of the user. It is apparent from this that there is a separate Desktop folder for each user, and any folders beneath that folder such as Autostart and Trash are also different for each user. The desktop of the "root" user is at /root/Desktop incidentally, and not off the /home directory.

Permissions

It is not just a matter of having personal KDE desktops for each user. This would still allow each user access to the files of every other user just by doing a bit of KFM navigation. As an experiment you could try logging in as "root" and placing one or two dummy files in Trash. There are graphics and text editing programs available via the "K" menu button that can be used to make dummy files, such as a drawing containing one line or a one-word text file. Having made the files and loaded them into Trash, logout of KDE and then login again as another user. If you now try to navigate your way to the /root/Desktop/Trash folder using KFM you will probably get no further than /root. Any attempt to get into the /root/Desktop folder should produce a window displaying an error message (Figure 4.1) stating that it was not possible to list the contents of the directory. This is not a bug in the system, and this is the way it is designed to work.

If you try things the other way round, with some files being placed in the Trash folder of an ordinary user, it will be possible to access them if you login as "root". You should be able to view and even edit them with a suitable program, and delete them from the system. If you login as an ordinary user you can only access the files which that user has permission

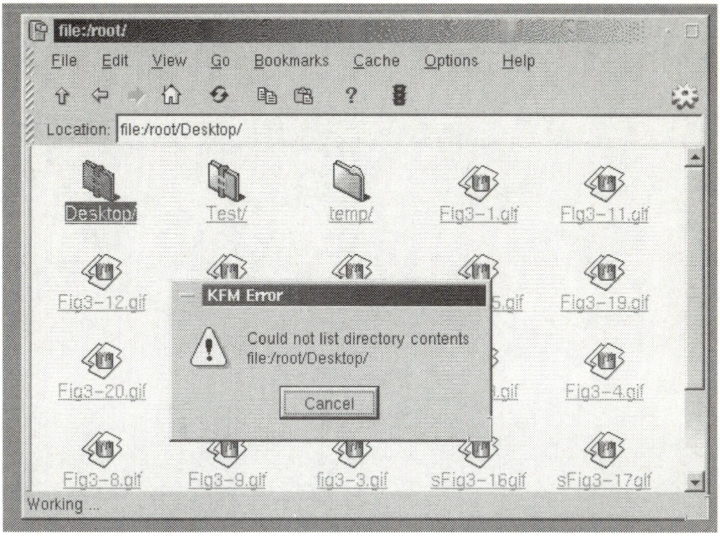

Fig.4.1 Some folders can only be accessed by privileged users

to access. Things are rather different if you login as "root", because this brings special privileges, and most things are possible for the "root" user. Details of permissions for a file or folder can be obtained by right-clicking on it in KFM, selecting Properties from the pop-up menu, and then left-clicking on the Permissions tag of the window that opens (Figure 4.2).

When a user is added to the system a number of things happen, and as we have already seen one of these is that a home directory for the user's files is generated. The user is also added to a database, and any files generated by that user are then marked as owned by that person. In addition to users there are groups, and the user will be added to at least one default user group. When a user logs-in to Linux the system decides what files he or she can access, and ensures that the user does not interfere with any files that are out of bounds. Things are different for the "root" user, who has full access and can alter permissions, add and delete users, etc. If we consider things at the most fundamental level, the Linux permissions system works in a quite straightforward manner. One user and one group own each file that is generated. There are nine switches that govern who can and can not access each file, and where appropriate the level of access available. This works on the basis of

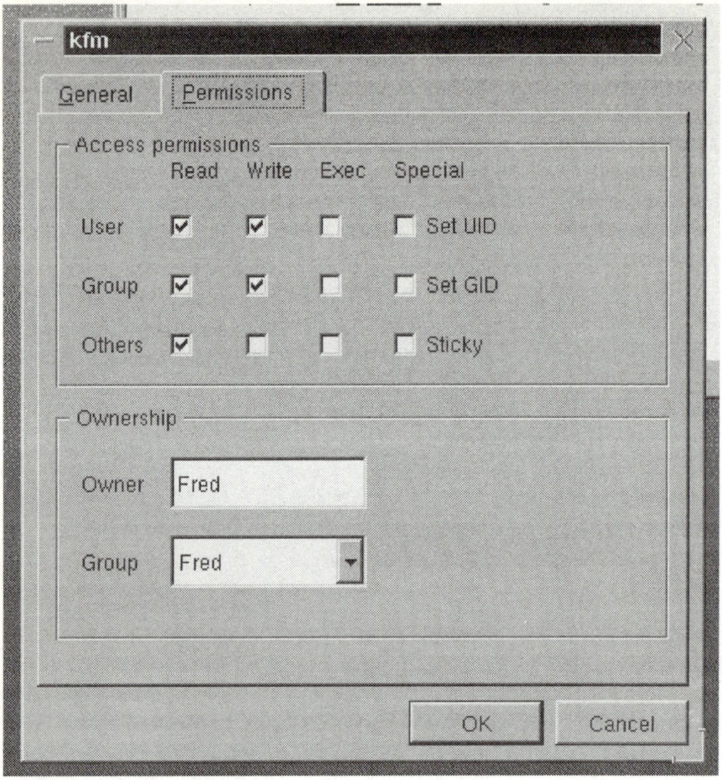

Fig.4.2 The KFM Permissions window

three access switches for each of three types of user. These are the user types.

Owner (User)

This will usually be the user who created the file. The owner has full control over permissions and can assign them as he or she thinks fit.

Group

The user is a member of a group associated with the file. Groups are needed where there are large numbers of users using the computer for different purposes. For example, one group might be involved with despatching goods, another group might deal with after sales, and another group could deal with the accounts, and so on. This is an easy way to give access to the people who need to use the file, but prevents access by all others. Each user can belong to any number of groups, but a file can only be associated with one group at a time.

Others

A user who does not own the file, and is not a member of a group related to the file.

These are the three switches.

Read (R)

This switch allows the contents of the file to be inspected, but does not permit its contents to be altered.

Write (W)

This switch permits the contents of the file to be altered, which includes deleting it altogether.

Execute (X)

In the case of a file, this switch permits the file to be run as a program. For a directory it enables the directory to be entered using the *cd* command, or opened in KFM or a similar program.

Files always have some permissions granted by default, and in normal use it will not usually be necessary to alter the permission settings. If a single operator uses the computer it should be possible to ignore this aspect of Linux, but if the computer is used by two or more operators you will probably need to exercise some control over permissions. The KFM permissions screen should now start to make sense. If we consider it in slightly simplified form we have an arrangement like this.

	Read	**Write**	**Execute**
User	On	On	Off
Group	On	Off	Off
Others	On	Off	Off

On the KFM permissions screen a tick means that the switch is on and that type of permission is active, and a blank box means that the switch is turned off. You toggle from one to the other by left-clicking on a box. The default settings for a file made by a normal user are as in the table shown here, with anyone able to read the file but only the user having permission to edit or erase it. Suppose that you were not happy with the default settings, and you decided to make the file totally inaccessible to Others, but you wanted anyone in the group to be able to edit it. The set-up would have to be changed, as in this modified table.

	Read	Write	Execute
User	On	On	Off
Group	On	On	Off
Other	Off	Off	Off

The Execute switch only applies to program files, and can be used to prevent unauthorised use of software. However, this is not something that is normally needed, and it is accesses to data files that you will wish to restrict to certain users.

Listing

If you wish to display permissions for a file when using the command line interpreter use the *ls* command with -l option, as in this example:

ls -l textdoc

Information on the file is displayed in the form of ten text characters. The first character is the file type, and is a hyphen for normal files. There is a range of letters for other types, such as "d" for directories and "l" for links. This leaves the next nine characters to represent the nine permission switches. This is the order in which they appear:

Owner Read

Owner Write

Owner Execute

Group Read

Group Write

Group Execute

Others Read

Others Write

Others Execute

The default for an ordinary data file would therefore be "-RW-R—R—". The other information provided are the Owner and Group names plus the date and time that the file was created or last modified. It is possible to change file permissions using the command line interpreter and the *chmod* command. This works on the basis of using numbers to represent each type of permission, with the total value for the required permissions being used in the command. These are the numbers and the type of permission each one represents:

Number	Permission Type
0	No permission at all
1	Execute permission
2	Write permission
4	Read permission

If a file had read and write permission but you needed to change it to a read-only file, a value of 4 would be used. Conversely, if the file was read-only but you wished to change it to a read and write file, a value of 6 would be used (4 + 2 = 6). Of course, there are three types of permission to deal with (Owner, Group, and Other), so the instruction must include three numbers in that order. To set the file "textdoc" as read/write for Owner, read-only for Group, and no permissions for Other, this command would be used:

```
chmod 640 textdoc
```

If you need to change permissions for two or three files at the same time, this is possible and just requires all the filenames to be included in the command (with a space between each one). Of course, the same level of permission will be set for all the files included in the command. This version of the command would also set permissions for the files called "text1" and "text2":

```
chmod 640 textdoc text1 text2
```

Changing permissions from the command line is not that difficult, but it is clearly easier using KDE and KFM. Where possible it is probably better to stick with KFM for this type of thing.

Other Switches

If you look at the Properties window in KFM you will notice that there are three further switches under the Special heading. The first of these is the Set User Identity (set UID) switch. The exact function of this seems a bit obscure, but the basic idea seems to be to set the ID of a running program to match that of the file, thus transferring permissions of the file owner to the program user. This can give the program user permissions that he or she does not normally have. The set GID works in a similar fashion, but with the group ID. This switch also has another use when it is used on a directory. Files placed in that directory are automatically given the group ID of the directory. This can be used to ensure that any file placed in the directory belonging to a group is made accessible to everyone in the group. This will happen even if the default group of the user is different to the group ID of the directory. The sticky bit is used to protect the files in a directory from deletion. When this switch is active it is only possible for the owner of the directory, the owner of the file, or the superuser to delete the file.

The sticky, set GUID, and set UID switches can be set from the command line with the *chmod* command. They respectively require 1000, 2000, and 4000 to be added to the number used in the command, and the other bits must be set at the same time. The other bits will all be switched off if you do not add the appropriate values to the number in the command, as they will all be set at zero. If we take the earlier *chmod* example and modify it to set the sticky bit as well, this command would result:

chmod 1640 textdoc

Again, it is much easier to use the Permissions window of KFM, which makes it easy to see the current settings as well as making it easier to alter settings. Of course, whether you use KFM or the command line to alter permission settings, it is only possible if you have the authority to do so. Without this authority you can see the settings in the KFM Permissions window (if you can get into the directory containing the file), but no changes can be made.

Adding a group

If you wish to change the user group for a file this can be accomplished using the KFM Permissions window. The bottom section of the window shows the name of the current group and has a menu of installed groups to choose from. If you need to assign a file to a new group the group must be added first, since it can not be generated from the KFM Permissions window. A group can be added at the command line using the *groupadd* command. Suppose you wish to add a group called "newgroup". This command could be used:

groupadd -g 1000 newgroup

You have to supply a group ID number that the system is not already using, but you should be safe here if you use a fairly high number. In this example 1000 has been used, but anything from about 600 to 65000 should do. The maximum permissible number is 65535, but one or two numbers at the top of this range might already be in use. It is therefore advisable to regard 65000 as the maximum usable number. Only a privileged user can use a system administration command such as *groupadd*, so you must login as "root" to use it.

Having made a new group it then has to be assigned to one or more users before it can be used. If we again take "Fred" as our example user, by default he will be assigned to user groups "Fred" and "users". Trying to assign a "Fred" generated file to the "newgroup" group is not possible in the Permissions window, because only groups "Fred" and "users" will be listed. You can check the groups to which a user belongs using the *groups* command at the command line. Using this command would check which groups "Fred" belongs to:

groups Fred

This would return this answer:

Fred : Fred users

"Fred" is the primary group for "Fred" the user, and "users" is the only secondary group. Suppose we wished to remove "users" and assign "Fred" to "newgroup" instead. These two commands would do the job:

usermod -d /home/Fred -m Fred

usermod -G newgroup Fred

The first command directs the system towards the correct directory and user, and the next command then sets the secondary and primary groups for that user. If more than one secondary group is required, include all the names with a comma (but no space) between each one. For instance, this command would have "newgroup" and "users" as secondary groups for "Fred", with "Fred" still as the primary group:

usermod -G newgroup,users Fred

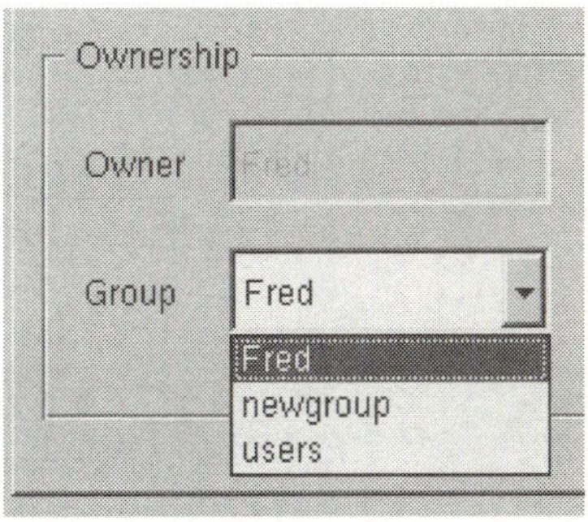

Fig.4.3 Selecting the group owning a file

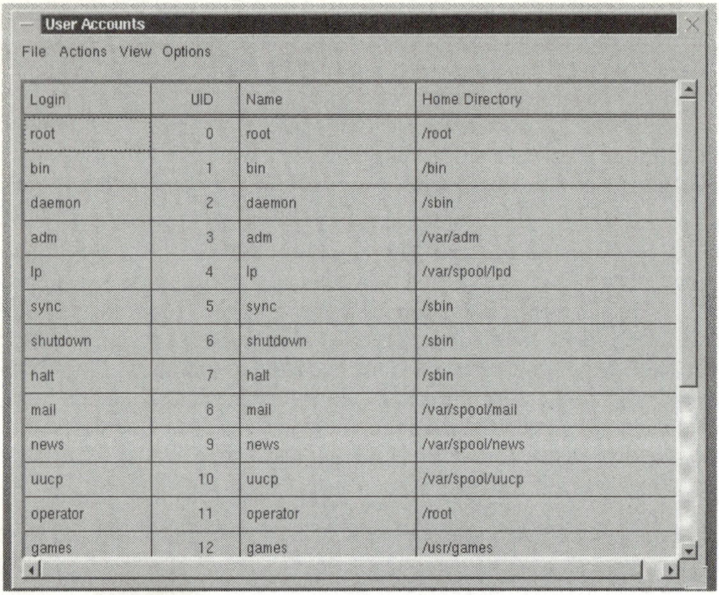

Fig.4.4 The COAS user accounts editing window

All three groups would then be available to a file owned by "Fred" (Figure 4.3). Of course, if you login as "root", all things are possible, and all the available groups will be available in the Permissions window. Any file can then be assigned to any group.

COAS

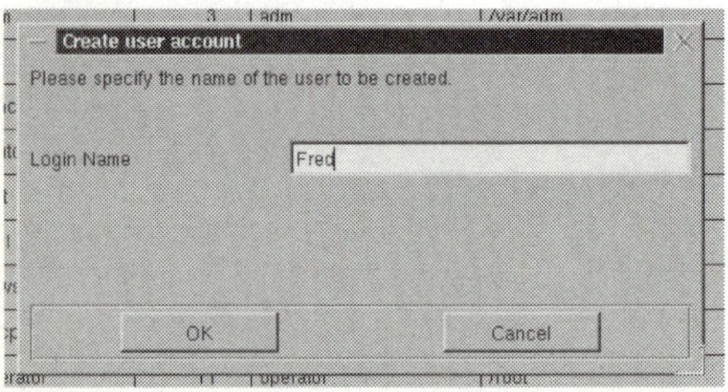

Fig.4.5 The account name edit box

Depending on the version and distribution of Linux you are using you may be able to administer user accounts via a graphical user interface. Caldera open Linux 2.2 has the COAS (Caldera

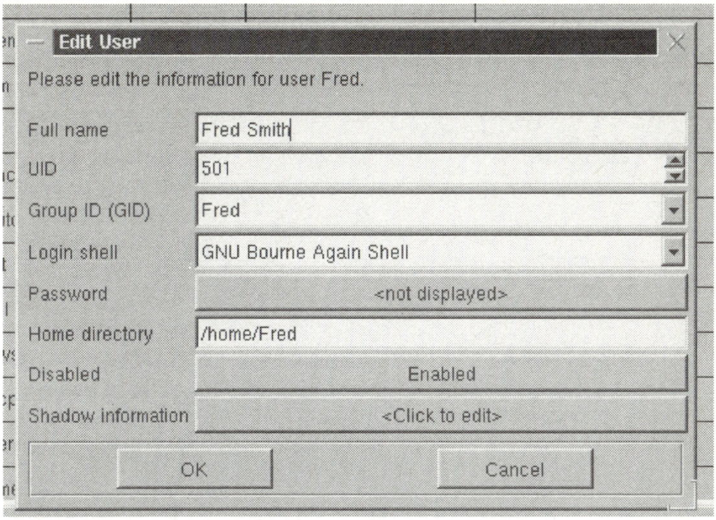

Fig.4.6 The form used to enter or edit account details

Open Administration System), which enables all manner of system settings to be viewed and controlled. To bring up the window that governs user accounts activate the "K" menu and then select COAS, System, and Accounts. This should bring up a window of the type shown in Figure 4.4. This initial screen enables some basic account details to be read, and the Actions menu permits accounts to be edited or created. If the Create option is selected, the login name for the new account is first entered into a dialogue box (Figure 4.5) and then other details such as the full name of the user and the password are added into the form that appears (Figure 4.6). Where possible, it is clearly easier to manage accounts using this sort of graphical front-end than it is via the command line.

KDE and discs

The way in which KDE handles discs is not quite the same in versions 1.0 and 1.1. In fact KDE 1.1 handles floppy discs and the CD-ROM in a much more convenient manner, and it is worth upgrading from 1.0 to 1.1 for this factor alone. As pointed out in chapter one, when running KDE 1.1 for the first time you are greeted by a Windows-style Wizard (Figure 4.7) and taken through a series of screens that enable the

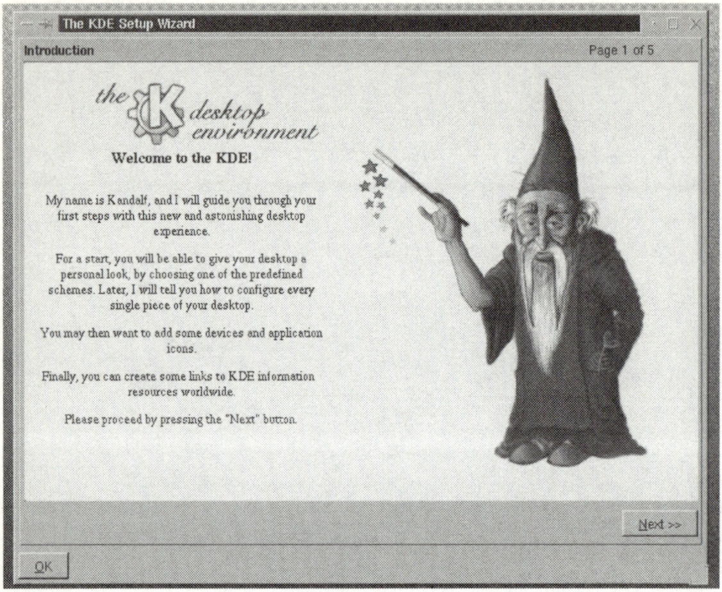

Fig.4.7 This wizard appears the first time KDE is run

program to be set up to suit individual preferences. One of these screens enables the user to select whether or not to have icons on the desktop for two floppy disc drives and the CD-ROM drive (Figure 4.8). I would strongly recommend having the icons as they make it very easy to access the floppy drives and the CD-ROM drive. Of course, if your computer does not have "floppy 2" (the equivalent of disc B in MS/DOS or Windows) you do not need the icon for this disc. If you did not have these icons added when KDE was first run, they can be added at a later date by running the KDE Wizard again. Operate the "K" button in the Panel, then select Utilities and KDE Configuration Wizard from the menu system.

If you do select the disc icons, the appropriate icons should be added to the desktop beneath the standard icons (Figure 4.9). Note that each user has a separate KDE desktop, and that this set-up process has to be repeated for each user. In order to access a standard CD-ROM you simply place it in the drive and then click on the CD-ROM icon. This will launch a KFM window that displays the contents of what is the root directory of the disc in MS/DOS and Windows terminology. In the Linux file system the CD-ROM is at /auto/cdrom, and not /mnt/cdrom as you might expect. This is not purely of academic importance, and this method

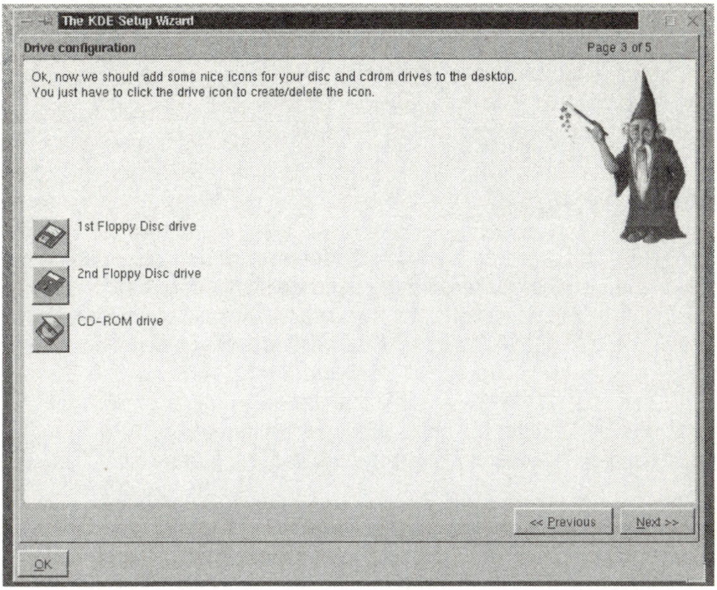

Fig.4.8 The easy way to add icons for discs in KDE 1.1

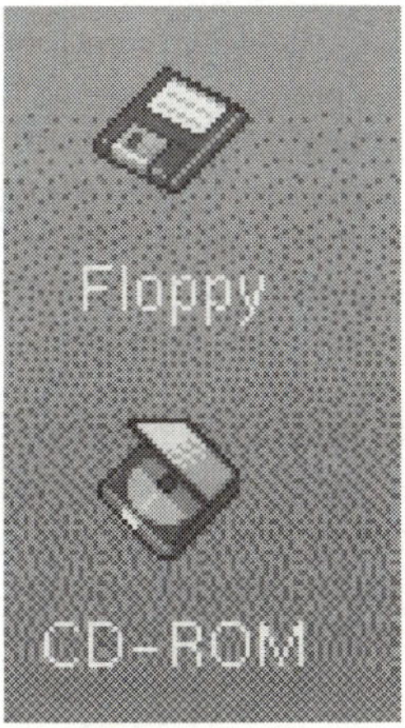

Fig.4.9 The added disc icons

of mounting the CD-ROM drive has definite advantages. There is no need to mount and unmount CD-ROMs. If you have finished with one CD-ROM and wish to use another, simply remove the first CD-ROM and replace it with the second one. If you then left-click on the Reload button the KFM window will change to show the contents of the new CD-ROM.

Things work in much the same way with floppy discs, and they are also placed in the file system at /auto/. You can freely change discs, and use them much as you would on a Windows system. When using an applications program you can save direct to the floppy disc by using /auto/floppy/filename. We are assuming here that only one floppy drive is present in the system. Where appropriate "floppy1" and "floppy2" must be used in place of just plain "floppy". You can also load from the floppy or

CD-ROM drives by using /auto/... as the path to the file. Do not use /mnt/floppy as the route to the floppy drive or use the *mount* and *umount* commands when the /auto/floppy route is in use. Similarly, if you are using /auto/cdrom to reach the CD-ROM drive do not use the /mnt/cdrom route, or try to mount or unmount the drive.

KDE 1.0 drives

If you use KDE 1.0 things are less straightforward. The disc icons have to be placed on the desktop by the user, which is not difficult. You can also do things this way in KDE 1.1 if you so wish, but it would seem to be pointless. Login and then run the KDE program. Right-click on a vacant area of the desktop and select New and then Device (or File System Device in KDE 1.1). In the window that appears (Figure 4.10) you must specify the filename for the icon, and you should replace "Device" in the default name with something appropriate, such as "Floppy" or "CDROM". Leave the ".kdelink" part of the filename unaltered. After you have exited this window a new icon will appear on the desktop, but so far it is not configured so it will only be a question mark at this stage. To configure the icon right-click on it and select Properties from the popup menu. In the window that appears (Figure 4.11) select the Device tab, and then in the Device box type "/dev/fd0" for a floppy disc icon or "/dev/cdrom" for a CD-ROM icon. Leave the other boxes untouched.

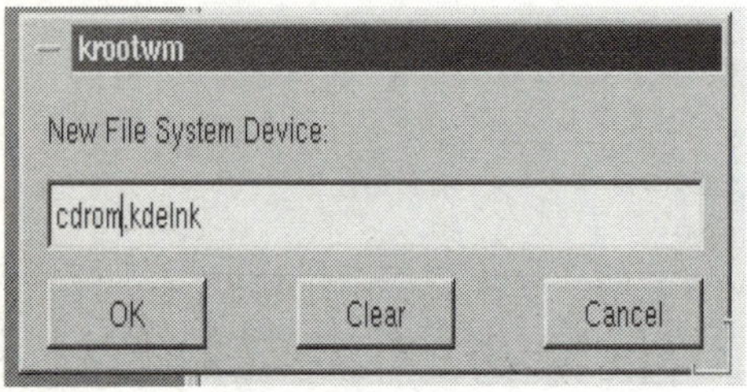

Fig.4.10 The edit box used to name the KDE link file

Next the icons for the device must be selected. It is a case of icons rather than icon because the icon displayed is different depending on whether the device is mounted or unmounted. To select the icons first left-click on the Mounted button near the bottom of the window. From the set of icons then shown choose the one that looks like a floppy disc with a small green square beside it, or its CD-ROM counterpart, as appropriate. Left-click on OK and then repeat the process using the Unmounted button, but choose the version of the icon that lacks the green square. This should give you something like Figure 4.12. Left-click on OK and the icon should change from the question mark to the unmounted disc version.

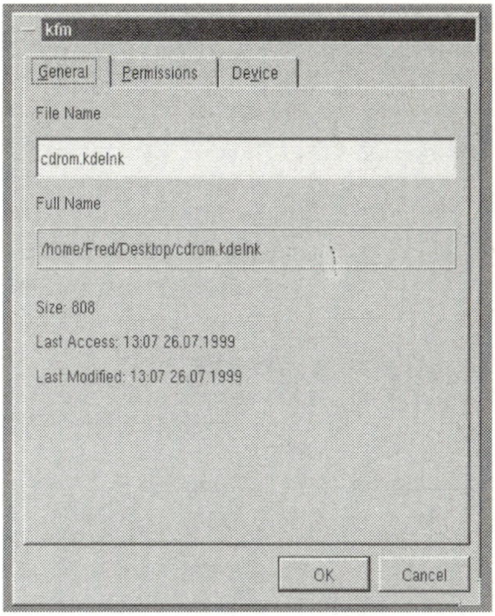

Fig.4.11 Setting the mount point for the drive

It is important to realise that once the icons are in place they can not be used in quite the same carefree manner as their KDE 1.1 counterparts. To use either the floppy drive or the CD-ROM drive first install a disc and then right-click on the appropriate icon. This produces a small popup menu from which the Mount option should be selected. The drive's icon should change from the plain version to the one with the green "light". You can then use the drive, and can left-click on its icon to view the contents using KFM. Files can then be copied, etc., in the usual way. When you have finished using the disc it should not simply be removed from the drive. In the case of the CD-ROM drive the door will probably be locked by the system, and it will not be possible to eject the disc anyway. Before a disc is removed it should be unmounted. To do this right-click on the drive's icon and then select Unmount from the popup menu. The icon should then change back to the plain version, and it is then safe to remove the disc.

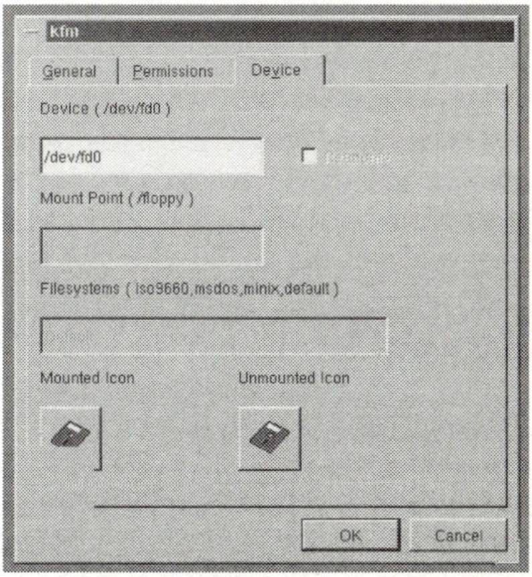

Fig.4.12 Choosing the drive icons

This is obviously far less convenient than using the floppy and CD-ROM drives in KDE 1.1. Also, depending on the default set-up of your system, setting up drives for other users than "root" to access in KDE might not be as easy. It will almost be necessary to edit the /etc/fstab file in order to make the drives available to non-privileged users, which is a bit risky. It is probably easier to upgrade to KDE version 1.1 than to use version 1.0!

Floppy formatting

A disc-formatting program will be needed if you need to format floppy discs. There seems to be no effective built-in disc formatting function available as standard at the command line. Fortunately, KDE does have a good disc-formatting program that can be accessed via the "K" menu button. If you select Utilities and then Kfloppy a window of the type shown in Figure 4.13 should appear. This program is very straightforward to use, and is similar to the disc formatting utility in Windows 95 and 98. There are Quick and Full options available, which respectively erase the disc and perform a full format of the disc. Only the Full option is usable with a disc that has not previously been formatted, or has been formatted to the wrong format. There is the option of DOS or Linux (ext2fs) formats. If you are using other PCs running MS/DOS or Windows it makes sense to use DOS format discs with KDE, as this makes it easy to swap data between the PCs. KDE will work quite happily with MS/DOS and Windows floppy discs, and should have no difficulty reading high or double density 3.5-inch discs produced using either of these operating systems. In fact KDE and the formatting program should be able to handle the older 5.25-inch discs, but I have never actually tried this. MS/DOS and Windows are unable to read from or write to Linux format discs.

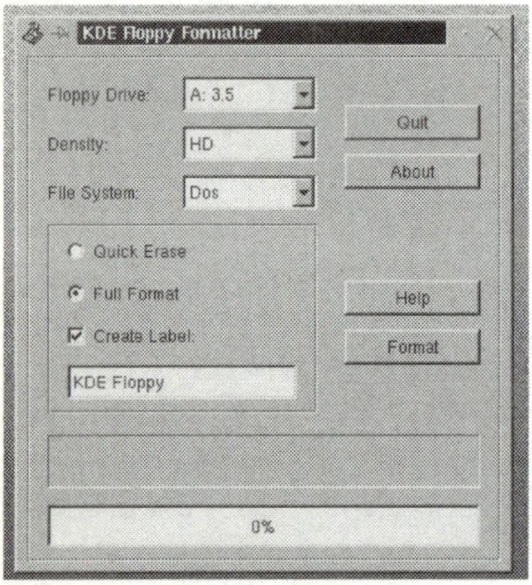

Fig.4.13 Formatting floppies is easy using Kfloppy

Customising KDE

Like most graphical user interfaces, KDE enables the user to customise the so-called "look and feel" of the desktop to suit individual requirements. Most users like to set the desktop background to suit their own tastes, and this is easy to do with KDE. Activate the "K" menu and the select Settings, Desktop, and Background. This will bring up a window that is

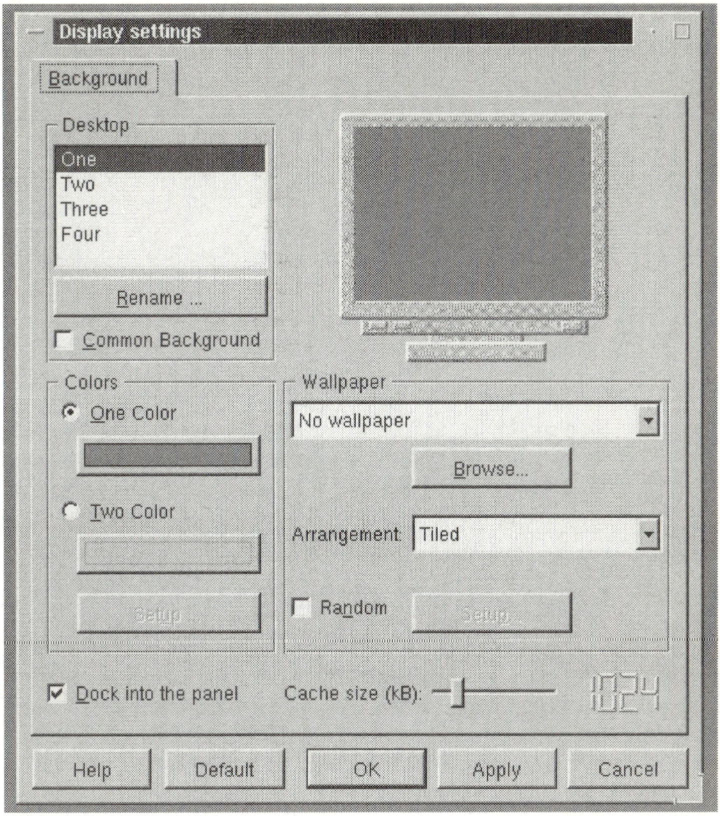

Fig.4.14 The screen used to make changes to the background

quite similar to its Windows 95 and 98 counterpart (Figure 4.14). You have the option of a single colour for the background, or a graduated two-colour effect. There are two bars that indicate the start and finish colours for a two-colour scheme, but one of these will be greyed-out if the single colour option is selected. Left-clicking on an active colour bar brings up the colour selection window (Figure 4.15), and the required colour can then be selected via a variety of means.

The main background selection window gives the option of using wallpaper, and dozens of different styles are on offer. Strangely, a "parrots" design is included in the standard range, but the Linux penguin is not. However, you can draw up your own because any JPEG image

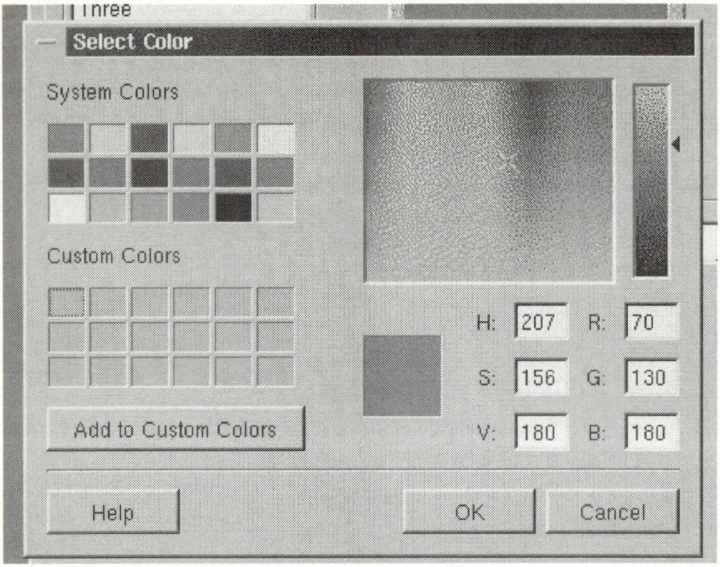

Fig.4.15 The background colour selection window

can be used as the wallpaper, and the standard range of effects (tiled, mirrored, scaled, etc.) can be applied to the wallpaper. The Browse option can be used to select a custom wallpaper image from anywhere in the file system, or the "root" user can copy the JPEG file into the /opt/kde/share/wallpaper directory. Photographing an old folding camera using a digital camera, and then using the "mirrored" wallpaper effect produced the vintage camera wallpaper design of Figure 4.16. By default the background settings will be applied to whatever virtual desktop the system is in at the time, but you can apply them to another one using the selection panel in the top left-hand corner of the settings window.

Adding desktops

By default there are four virtual desktops, but you might need more or less than this depending on the way you work with the computer. KDE enables each user to have up to eight virtual desktops, and it is quite easy to alter the number. Activate the "K" menu and then select Panel and Configure. This brings up the control panel shown in Figure 4.17, which gives a large degree of control over the Panel. The first of the four control panels governs such things as the position of the panel and its

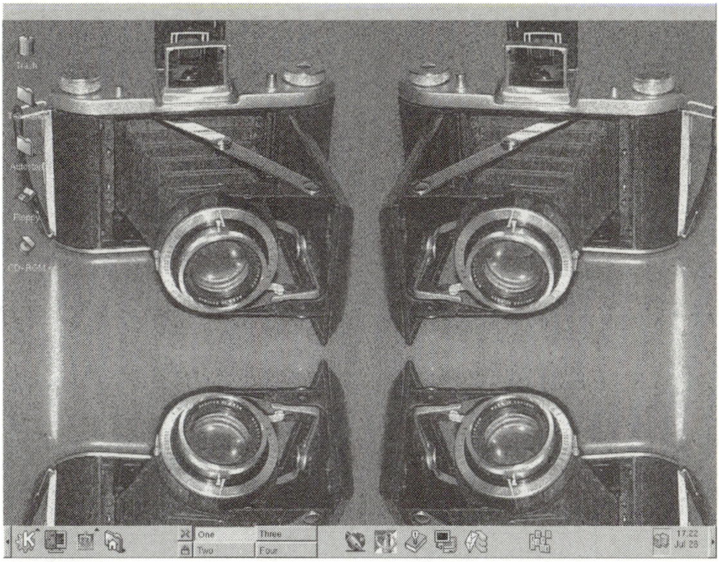

Fig.4.16 Home-made wallpaper added to the KDE desktop

size. To alter the number of virtual desktops left-click on the Desktops tab to bring up the control panel shown in Figure 4.18. The upper of the two slider controls (labelled Visible) enables the number of virtual desktops to be altered. Drag it to the right to increase the number of desktops, or to the left to decrease the number. Only even numbers of desktops are allowed, so there is a choice of two, four, six, or eight.

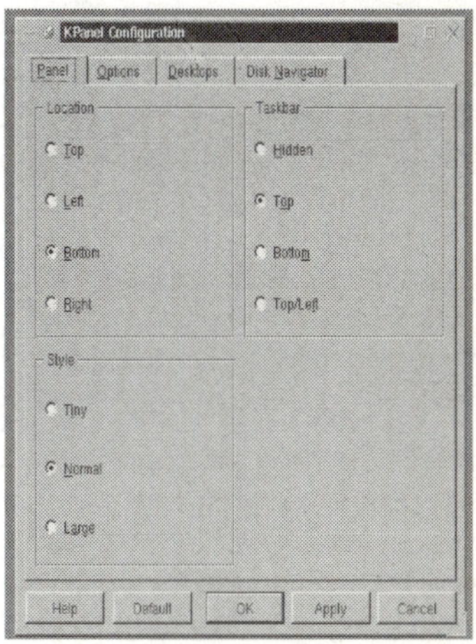

Fig.4.17 Controlling the size and position of the Panel

This panel also enables each desktop to be renamed using the edit boxes. You could give the virtual desktops appropriate names such as “Spreadsheet” and “Graphics” instead of the default “One”, “Two”, etc. The lower slider control marked “Width” controls the width of the desktop selection buttons on the panel. This must be set wide enough

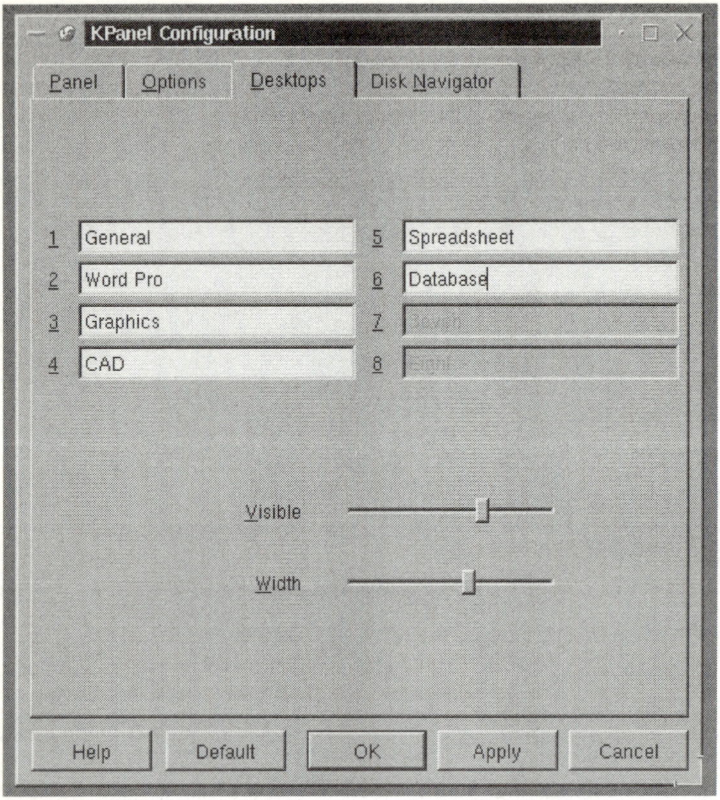

Fig.4.18 The upper slider controls the number of desktops

to accommodate the legends, but it obviously makes sense to keep the buttons as narrow as possible to leave as much space as possible for other buttons on the panel. You can operate the Apply button to see if everything looks right before exiting from the Desktops control panel.

Border controls

It is possible to have automatic switching between desktops if desired. This works on the basis of automatically switching to the next desktop if you move the pointer to an appropriate edge of the screen. The relative positions of the virtual desktops match up with their buttons on the panel.

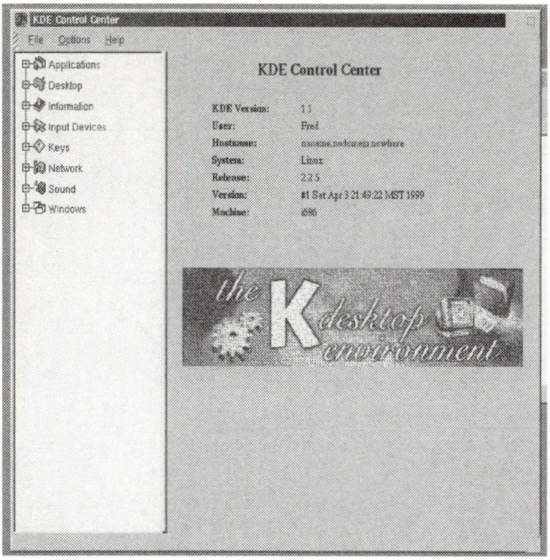

Fig.4.19 The KDE Control Centre main window

If the system is in desktop One and you move a window so that the pointer touches the right-hand side of the screen, the automatic switching would take the system into desktop Three, and would continue operating normally from there. If the pointer touched the bottom of desktop One the system would switch automatically to desktop Two. Taking the pointer to the extreme left-hand side or the top of the screen would have no effect, since there are no virtual desktops in those directions. The automatic switching effectively combines the virtual desktops into one huge desktop, which might seem like the ideal way of doing things. In practice it is one of those features that you either love or hate. If you are suitably precise with your control of windows it can work very well, but if not you can find yourself accidentally switching from one desktop to another on a fairly regular basis!

This automatic switching is called the Active Desktop Borders feature, and is enabled via the KDE Control Center Application. Activate this program by way of the KDE Control Center option in the "K" menu. This will bring up the window shown in Figure 4.19. Next left-click on the plus sign next to "Desktop" to show the sub-options, and the select Borders. This will open the control panel shown in Figure 4.20, and Active Borders can then be enabled by left-clicking on the appropriate check box. You then have the further option of having the pointer move towards the centre after each switch, and there is also an adjustable delay before the switchover occurs. Using a delay slows things down, but it can help to avoid accidentally switching from one desktop to another. I would definitely recommend using at least a short delay.

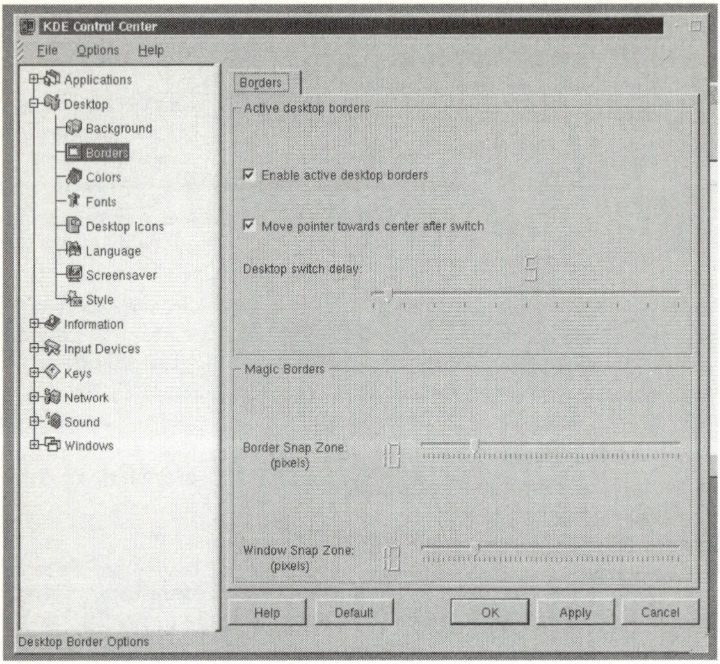

Fig.4.20 Setting active borders in the KDE Control Center

Using the Active Borders feature you can move a window from one desktop to another by dragging it to an edge of the screen. When the pointer hits the edge of the screen the system moves on to the next desktop, taking the window with it. Another method of switching a window from one desktop to another is to select Desktop from the Window menu, and then select the required desktop from the fly-out submenu.

Desktop Pager

The Desktop Pager application offers another way of moving a window from one desktop to another. To run this program, activate the "K" menu and then select the System and Desktop Pager options. This should result in a small window opening in the bottom left-hand corner of the screen just above the Panel (Figure 4.21). If you are only using two virtual desktops this window will show thumbnail views for both of them.

Fig.4.21 The KDE Desktop Pager

If the system is set for four or more desktops only the first two will be shown in the thumbnail views, but by left-clicking on the arrows it is possible to scroll along to the other desktops, and back again. Alternatively, the window can be dragged to a different size in the usual way, and if a suitable aspect ratio is selected all the desktops will be visible. By double clicking on a thumbnail the system is moved into that desktop.

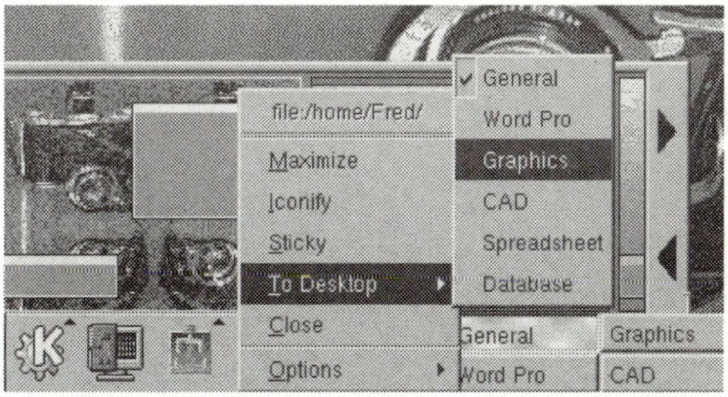

Fig.4.22 The window menu is available from the Desktop Pager

The thumbnail views only show each window as a grey rectangle, and show no details of the contents. However, you can find basic details of a window by right-clicking on it. This will bring up the window menu for that window, complete with the contents of the window's title bar at the top of the menu. To move a window from one desktop to another it is again a matter of right-clicking on the representation of the window in the Desktop Pager, which will bring up the window menu. It is then just a matter of switching windows in the usual fashion. First select Desktop from the menu and then select the required desktop from the fly-out menu (Figure 4.22). All the other options in the window menu operate in the normal fashion incidentally.

If you want to close the Desktop Pager, first right-click within its window, but not on an area that represents a window on a desktop. This brings up a menu with various options for the Desktop Pager itself. Select the Show Menubar option, which will put the usual menu bar at the top of the window. To close the program, activate the File menu and then choose the Quit option.

Auto-restore

When using KDE you will soon notice that it tends to start up where it left off. Any programs that were left running when you logged out will probably be restored onto the relevant desktop, much as you left them, next time you login. This auto-restore feature works better with some programs than with others. It works best with KDE-aware programs, and will work with most X11-aware software, but is unlikely to work at all with any console applications. If you try to logout without saving any data that KDE can not restore it will produce a warning message to that effect. It is good practice to always save data before logging out anyway, and it is not a good idea to assume that KDE will restore everything next time you login, just in case it is unable to do so.

Panel icons

There are some program icons on the Panel by default, but you can add your own. Suppose you wished to add icons for the Asteroids and Mahjongg games. The first task is to locate the relevant program files using KFM, and this is potentially a little difficult as they are buried quite deep in the file structure. The *locate* command is often helpful in a situation such as this, but you should find both files in the /opt/kde/bin folder. To place buttons for these programs on the Panel, complete with suitable icons (Figure 4.23), simply drag the program icons from KFM and onto a vacant area on the Panel. This will leave the program files intact, but will produce links to them via the buttons on the Panel. To run one of the programs simply left-click on its button, just like launching any other program from the Panel. Note that this will only work with KDE and X11 software, and can not be used to run console applications.

Fig.4.23 The added icon

There is an alternative method of adding buttons to the Panel for the programs in the "K" menu. Activate the "K" menu and then select Panel and Add Application. You then select the relevant program from the fly-out menu, which is more or less a clone of the "K" menu structure. You end up quite deep in a menu structure (Figure 4.24), but once you have selected the program its button is automatically added to the Panel.

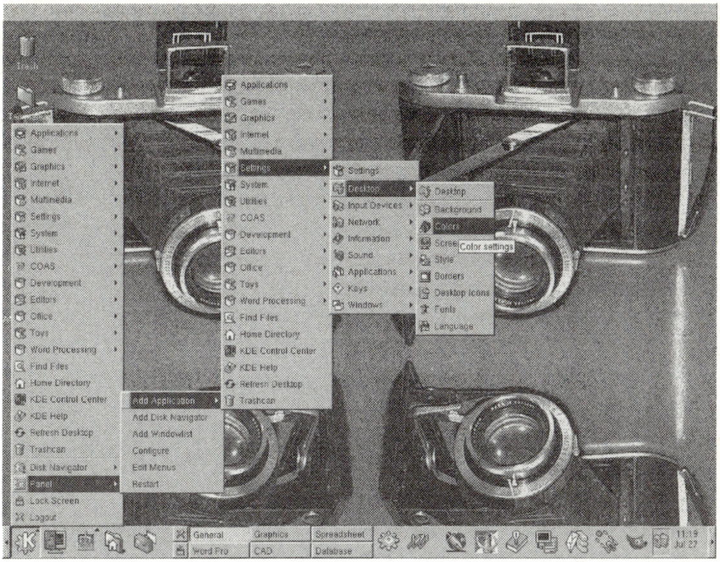

Fig.4.24 Adding a Panel icon using a clone of the main "K" menu

In order to remove a button from the Panel right-click on the button and then select Remove from the popup menu (Figure 4.25). The Move option in this menu has nothing to do with moving the program file or the link to it. This option enables the button to be moved along the Panel to the required location using the mouse. You may like to use this option to relocate some of the default buttons. The Properties option brings up what is more or less the usual Properties window, detailing permissions, etc.

Fig.4.25 Removing a Panel icon

Program icons

As pointed out in the previous chapter, you can put an icon for a program or a file onto the desktop simply by dragging it from KFM and then selecting the Link option. This method is quick and easy but does not give any control over the icon. The alternative route is to do things in

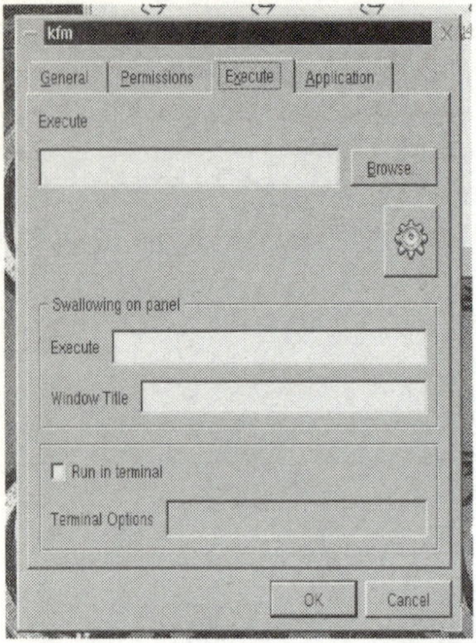

Fig.4.26 The Browse option makes it easy to find the right file

much the same way as adding a device icon to the desktop, which was described previously in this chapter. Right-click on an empty section of the desktop and then select New and Application. This brings up a small dialogue box into which you type a suitable name for the program where it currently says "Program". Leave the ".kdelink" part of the name unaltered. This part of the name tells the system that the file you are creating is KDE link file.

This puts a default gearwheel icon on the desktop, but as yet it will not actually do anything. To tell the system the location of the program file, right-click on the icon and select Properties from the popup menu. Next left-click on the Execute tab to bring up the form shown in Figure 4.26. If you know the path and filename for the program, it can be typed into the Execute edit box. Even if you do, you may prefer to use the Browse option to select the program file. If you would like to select an alternative to the gearwheel icon, left-click on the gearwheel icon on this form and select a different one from the window that then opens (Figure 4.27). The gearwheel icon should then change to the one you have selected. Finally, left-click on OK to exit the Properties window, and then left-click on the program icon to check that it launches the program properly.

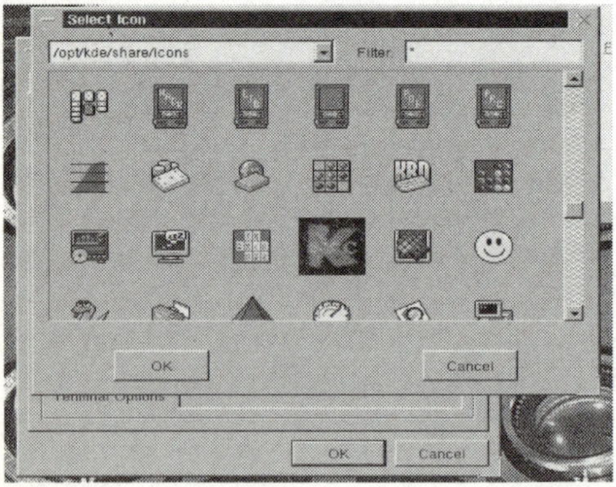

Fig.4.27 Choosing an icon for the program

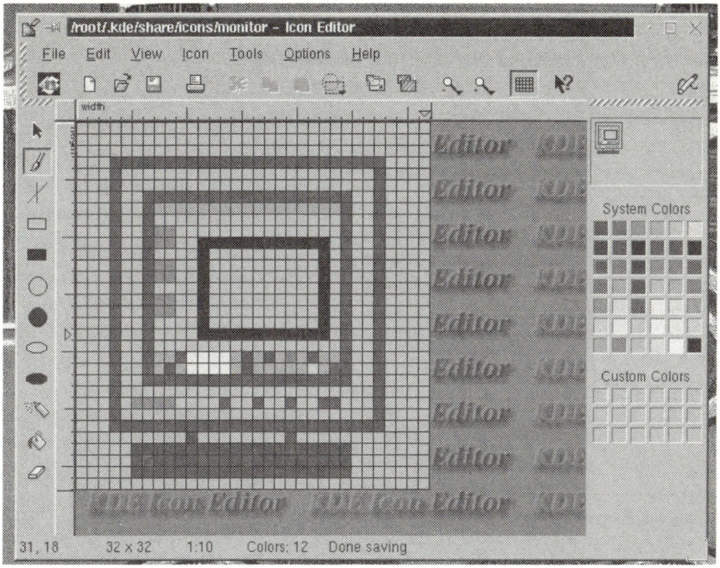

Fig.4.28 DIY icons can be produced using the Icon Editor application

DIY icons

If you feel like producing your own icons there is a good icon editor program available via the "K" menu. Selecting graphics and then Icon Editor will launch the icon editing and creation program (Figure 4.28). The icons have to be quite small at only 32 pixels by 32 pixels, so do not try to be too detailed when drawing your own. You can draw some primitive shapes using the drawing tools down the left-hand side of the window, but with simple graphics such as icons it is often easier just to add things one pixel at a time using the paintbrush tool. To select a drawing colour simply left-click on the required colour in the palette towards the right-hand side of the window. Once a masterpiece is complete it should be saved to the /opt/kde/share/icons folder with an "xpm" extension. KDE will then be able to locate you new icon, and when you browse through the program icons in the Properties window it should be included with the standard icons. It can then be selected and used just like any other icon.

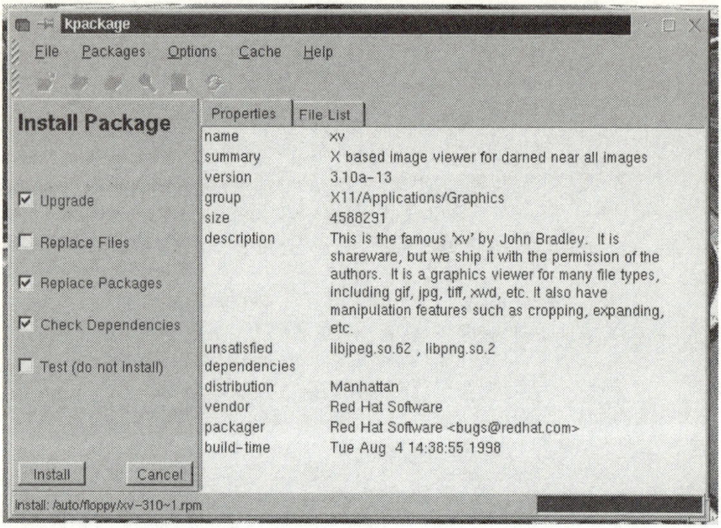

Fig.4.29 Installing an RPM package using Kpackage

KDE and RPM

As pointed out in chapter 2, these days many Linux applications are distributed in the form of RPM files. KDE includes an application called Kpackage for dealing with RPM files, and this can be activated by left-clicking on a RPM file in KFM. This brings up the window shown in Figure 4.29. The five check boxes towards the left of the window enable various options to be selected, such as checking or not checking dependencies, and whether or not files should be overwritten. Once the required options have been selected, left-clicking on the Install button either results in the software being installed, or error messages explaining what has gone wrong.

Kpackage is available via the "K" menu by selecting Utilities and then Kpackage. This gives a somewhat different screen (Figure 4.30), and in this form it is intended for uninstalling rather than installing software. It is still possible to install software from this screen, and it is just a matter of activating the File menu and selecting Open. The appropriate RPM file is then located and opened, which then gives you a window of the type shown in Figure 4.29. The software is then installed from here in the usual way.

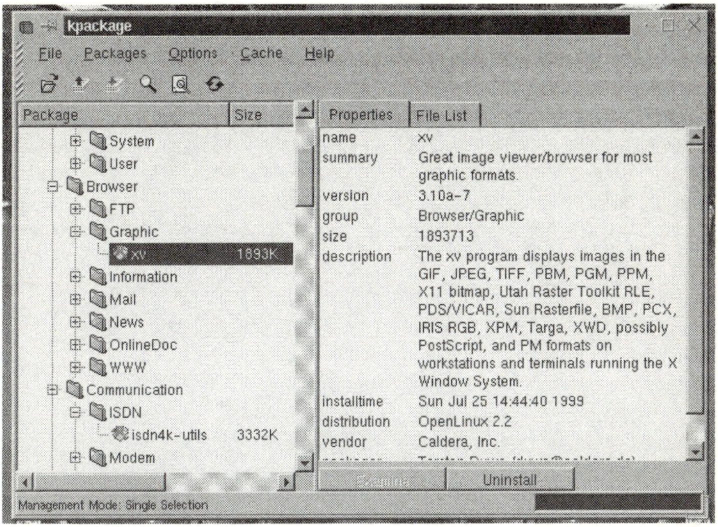

Fig.4.30 Using Kpackage to uninstall software

When used to uninstall software, the tree at the left-hand side of the screen shows various software categories and sub-categories. Double clicking on one of these expands it to show the contents. Having located the program you wish to remove, left-clicking on it brings up details of the program in the main window area. The Uninstall button becomes active, and left-clicking on it will result in the program being removed. You will get a chance to change your mind before the uninstall procedure starts, so there is little risk of accidentally uninstalling anything. If you should accidentally remove something or simply change your mind, it should be possible to locate the RPM file on the installation disc and simply reinstall it from CD-ROM using Kpackage.

Unzip

KFM can handle zipped tar files, but it does not seem to do as well with MS/DOS and Windows files that have been zipped using a program such as Winzip or PKunzip. These files usually have "zip" as the extension. If you left-click on a file of this type it will launch the Archiver program, which will then display the contents of the zipped file (Figure 4.31). The contents of text files can be read by clicking on the relevant file in the list, and it seems to be possible to extract some files. If extracting

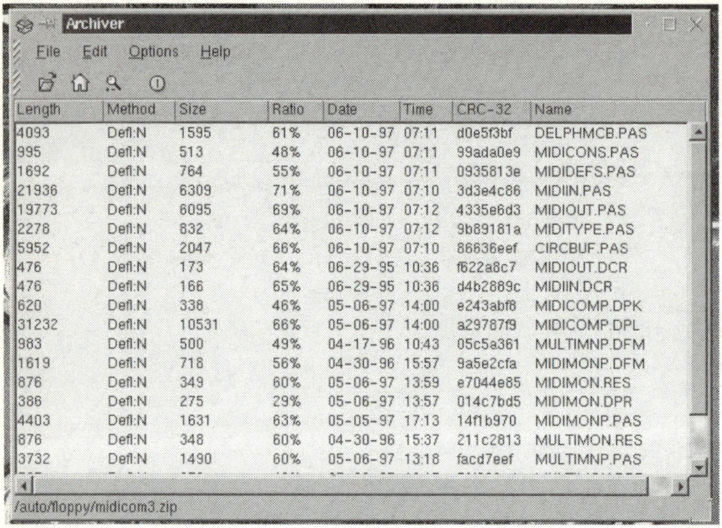

Fig.4.31 The contents of a zip file displayed by the Archiver application

files using the Archiver program proves to be impossible then it should be possible to do so via the command line and the *unzip* command. To use this command, just include the name of the file to be unzipped at the end of the command. Use the complete filename including the "zip" extension. For example, this command would extract the files within the file called "testfile.zip":

unzip testfile.zip

The "testfile.zip" file would have to be in the current directory, and the unzipped files would be placed in that directory. There are plenty of options available with the *unzip* command, but for most purposes this basic form is all that is needed. Use this command if you require a list of the available options:

unzip —help

Memory

If you limit yourself to running one application at a time it is unlikely that the amount of free memory will be a consideration unless you are trying to get by with the bare minimum. If you make a habit of running several applications at once the amount of free memory becomes more significant. From within KDE it is possible to use one of the system information programs to get information on the amount of free memory and the way the computer's memory is allocated. Activate the "K" menu and then select Settings, Information, and Memory. This will bring up an information window of the type shown in Figure 4.32. This monitor program will continue to update its figures even when it is not the active window, so you can run various programs and note their effect on memory usage. The more programs that you run the lower the figure for "Free memory" will become.

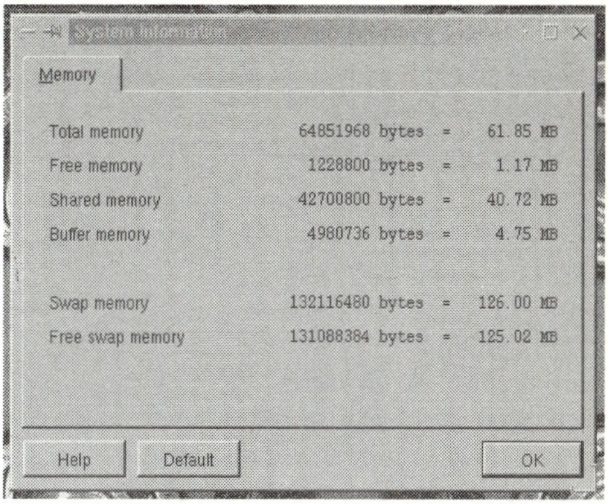

Fig.4.32 Memory information obtained from one of KDE's information utilities

Fig.4.33 Memory information obtained via the command line

It is also possible to obtain some facts and figures about memory usage from the command line interpreter. The most basic command line utility for monitoring memory is the *free* command, and to use it you simply type in this command:

free

This provides much the same information as its KDE equivalent, including a figure for the amount of free memory (Figure 4.33).

There are other system monitoring programs available via the "K" menu and the Settings - Information route, including information about the processor. This will tell you the processor clock speed to the nearest hertz, and all sorts of other facts and figures.

Free disc space

Information on free disc space is something that most users need to keep under scrutiny, and this information can be obtained via the command line interpreter. If you simply need to know how much free space there is on the hard disc use the *df* (disc free) command. This can be used without any option flags, as in this example:

df

The ds command will respond with four figures which are the total disc capacity in kilobytes, the number of kilobytes used, the number of kilobytes free, and the percentage of the disc that is actually used. The third figure is therefore the all-important one that tells you how much disc space is free. Divide this figure by 1000 to get the approximate amount of free disc space in megabytes. It is not possible to go on putting more and more small files onto the disc forever. Eventually the limit will be reached even if the disc has some unused space. Frankly, the chances of this happening are about the same as winning the jackpot on the lottery, but you can check the current state of things using the *df* command and the -i (inode) option, like this:

df -i

This gives four figures, as before, but this time it is the total number of available inodes, the number used, the number free, and the percentage used. On my PC the disc is 54 percent full, but only 12 percent of the available inodes are used, so it is normally the disc capacity that runs out first.

The *du* (disc usage) command is another command line disc utility which could be useful. It shows how much disc space (in kilobytes) each directory occupies. If there are directories beneath the specified directory the space occupied by these will be listed as well (Figure 4.34). In its basic form the *du* command provides a listing for the current directory, plus any subdirectories. If you require a listing for some other directory simply specify the directory at the end of the command. This example produces a listing for /home/Fred and its subdirectories:

du /home/Fred

A size for a file can be obtained simply by specifying a file rather than a

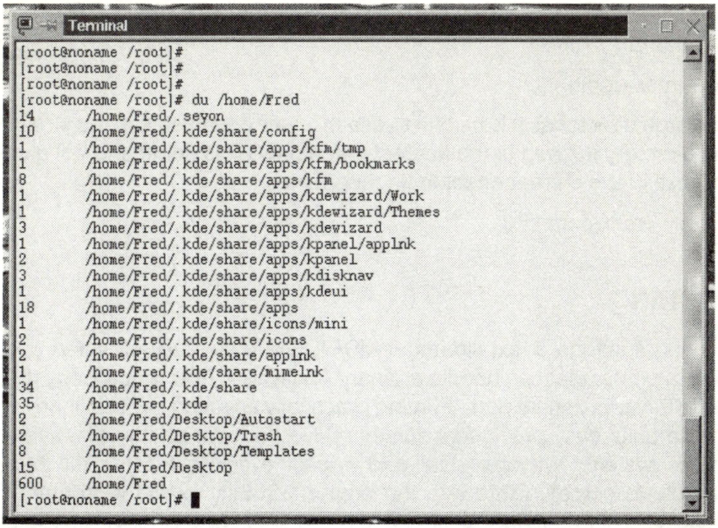

Fig.4.34 Directory information obtained from the disc usage program

directory. This example would give the size of the file called "testfile" in the current directory:

du testfile

Note that the size of a file can be determined from within KDE by locating the file using KFM, right-clicking on its icon, and then selecting Properties from the popup menu. The file size will be included on the first screen of information. Alternatively, simply placing the pointer over a file icon will give its size in the status line at the bottom of the KFM window. Unfortunately neither method works with a directory. The Properties window with simply say "Is a Directory" instead of giving a size, and the status line will just say "Folder".

There are various option flags that can be used with the *du* command, and this command will bring up a list of them:

du —help

The "—max-depth=N" option is a useful one if you only require details of the current directory, and are not interested in subdirectories several levels beneath it. This command will list the size of the current directory and the sub-directories immediately below it:

du —max-depth=1

If you only need to know the size of the current directory use this command:

du —max-depth=0

For large directories it is helpful to use the "-m" option so that the size of the directory is given to the nearest megabyte. This command will give the size of the current directory in megabytes:

du -m —max-depth=0

Printing

Printing a standard text file under MS/DOS is quite easy provided you have a printer that can handle ordinary ASCII files. You simply copy the file to the appropriate port. Printing practically anything under Windows is also quite easy provided a suitable driver for your printer is installed on the system. Windows itself and virtually every application will then be able to communicate with the printer and fully exploit it (in theory anyway). Things are far less straightforward under Linux, but it is possible to output direct to the printer. Whether you would ever need to do so and how much good it would do you is questionable. Most of the files you wish to print out will be produced using an application such as Applix, StarOffice, or WordPerfect, all of which have their own ways of dealing with the printer. Some applications programs such as WordPerfect will operate with a wide range of printers, but others will only print out to a PostScript compatible printer. It is really a matter of taking each application as it comes.

Applications programs might go totally their own way with the handling of the printer, but it is advisable to have the printer properly installed in Linux anyway. This will normally be included in the installation process, but it is possible to add or alter the printer configuration later. There is more than one installation and configuration program in use, but with most systems the LISA (Linux Installation and Administration) program is used. Where appropriate use the alternative configuration program supplied with you Linux distribution. LISA can be run from the command line using this command:

LISA

You should then be greeted with the screen shown in Figure 4.35. It is possible to reconfigure all manner of things using LISA, but to get to the printer control panel select the System Configuration, Hardware

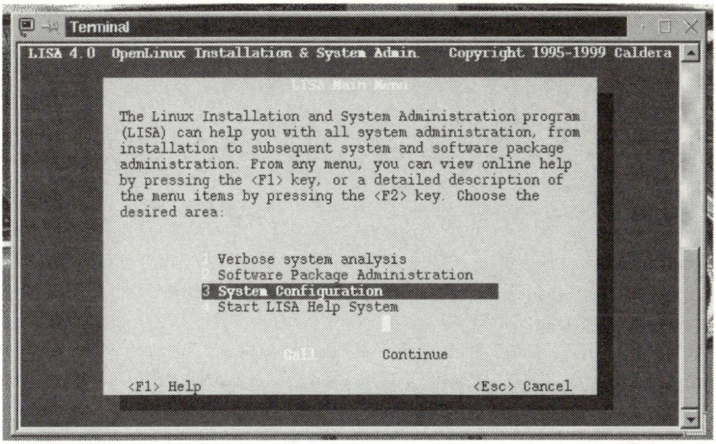

Fig.4.35 The initial screen when LISA is run

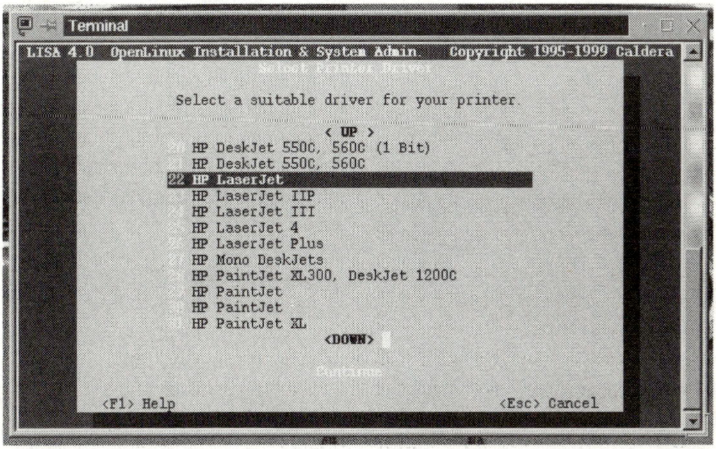

Fig.4.36 Selecting the printer type from the list provided

Configuration, and Configure Printer options. You will then be able to choose from a long list of printers (Figure 4.36). Use the up and down cursor keys to scroll through the list and highlight the correct one, and then press the Return key to select it. Further screens then enable the appropriate port to be selected (Figure 4.37), and there will probably be further screens to select such things as the default printing resolution

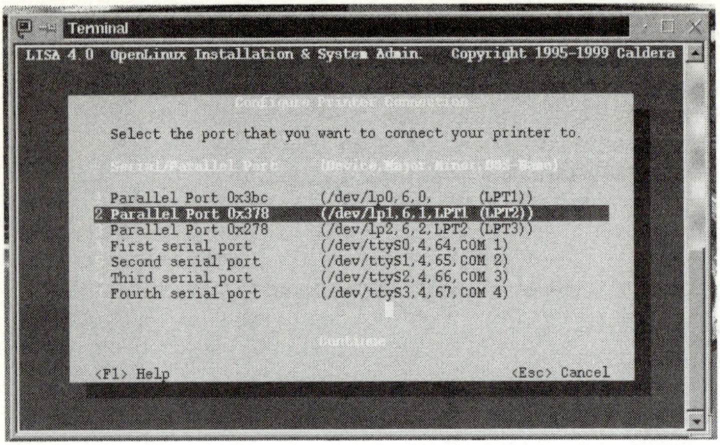

Fig.4.37 Selecting the correct port for the printer

and the paper size. Once this has been completed press the Escape key to exit LISA and the printer is then ready for use.

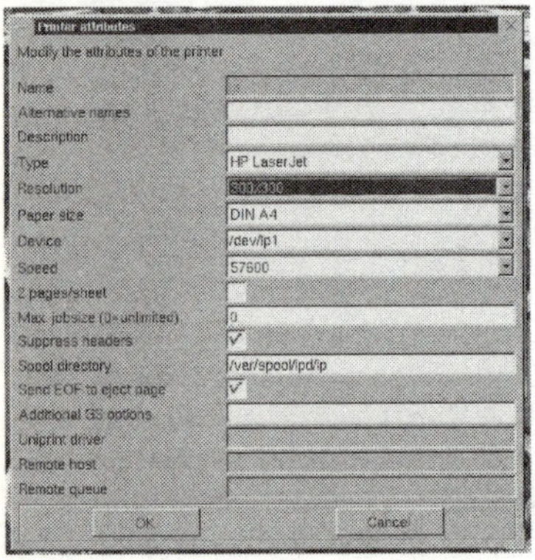

Fig.4.38 COAS printer configuration

It might be possible to configure the printer using KDE and a graphical used interface. Caldera Open Linux 2.2 has the COAS system mentioned previously. To add or reconfigure a printer, activate the "K" menu and then select the Peripherals and Printer options. This brings up a small window that enables printers to be added or existing configurations to be edited. Using either option opens another window that permits easy configuration of the printer (Figure 4.38).

Direct printing

It is possible to print direct from the printer from the command line, and it is just a matter of copying the file to whichever port the printer is connected to. This will usually be in the file system at /dev/lp0, so to

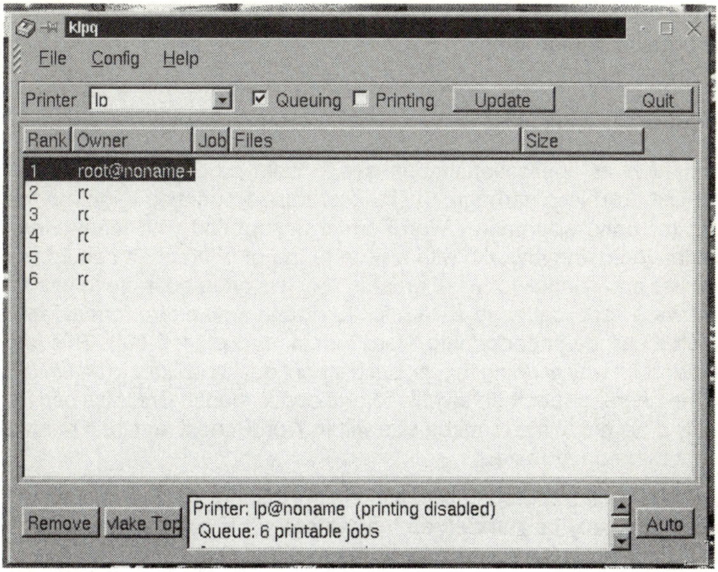

Fig.4.39 Printing via the Printer Queue utility

copy the text file "text1" in the current directory to the printer this command would be used:

cp text1 /dev/lp0

This will probably work quite well if the printer understands ASCII text and the file you are copying is a simple ASCII text file and not something like a graphics file or a text file having embedded formatting instructions. However, do not be surprised if there are the usual problems with form-feeds and line spacing that tends to dog basic text printing. The KDE equivalent of direct printing is to use the Prinert Queue utility that can be launched from the "K" menu by selecting Utilities and Printer Queue. If you have opted for a printer icon on the desktop, then just left-click on the printer icon to launch the Printer Queue utility. Either way, the window of Figure 4.39 should appear. Files dragged from KFM to the main area in this window will be printed, but again this is only usable with simple text files and a suitable printer. Of course, it will also work with any files that have been specifically produced for your type of printer. It should even work with graphics or mixed text and graphics files that have been formatted to suit the printer. Using the check boxes at the top of the screen you can opt to have files printed immediately or queued. The buttons at the bottom of the window enable files to be removed from the print queue or reordered.

Indirect printing

If you have an application that refuses to "talk" properly to your printer and just produces garbage, the indirect route to printing might be the best (or only) approach. WordPerfect is supplied with many Linux distributions, and it works with a wide range of printers. It can import text files and various forms of graphic file. It is often possible to use an "awkward" application to save a file to disc in a standard format, after which it can be imported into WordPerfect, and printed out. This is a roundabout way of doing things, but the print quality is likely to be limited by the printer rather than any file format conversions. Graphics can be easily dragged to the required size within WordPerfect and then printed out at the required size..

Another indirect approach is to use the *ghostscript* application that will almost certainly be installed on the system. This program can take a PostScript file and convert it into output that is suitable for a range of popular printers such as Hewlett Packard DeskJets, LaserJets, and compatibles. Many Linux applications can "print" their PostScript output to a file on the hard disc, and can therefore be made to drive a range of non-PostScript printers via *ghostscript*. If *ghostscript* is on the system there will be a lot of documentation for it at /usr/share/ghostscript/5.10/doc. The 5.10 part of this path is the version number, and will be different if you are not using version 5.10.

This is a command line utility, and it is not the most straightforward of programs to use. I find the easiest way to use it is to send the output to a file, and to then print that file via the Printing Queue utility. Suppose that you have a PostScript file in the current directory called Picture.ps and you wish to produce a LaserJet printer file called Print.prn. This command would have the desired effect:

gs -sDEVICE=laserjet -sOutputFile=Print.prn Picture.ps

Be careful to use upper and lower case letters in the appropriate places. Having a printer file is convenient if you will need to print the document again later, but otherwise there should be no problem in sending the output direct to the printer, as in this version of the command:

gs -sDEVICE=laserjet -sOutputFile=/dev/lp0 Picture.ps

Of course, if the printer is at other than /dev/lp0 the appropriate path

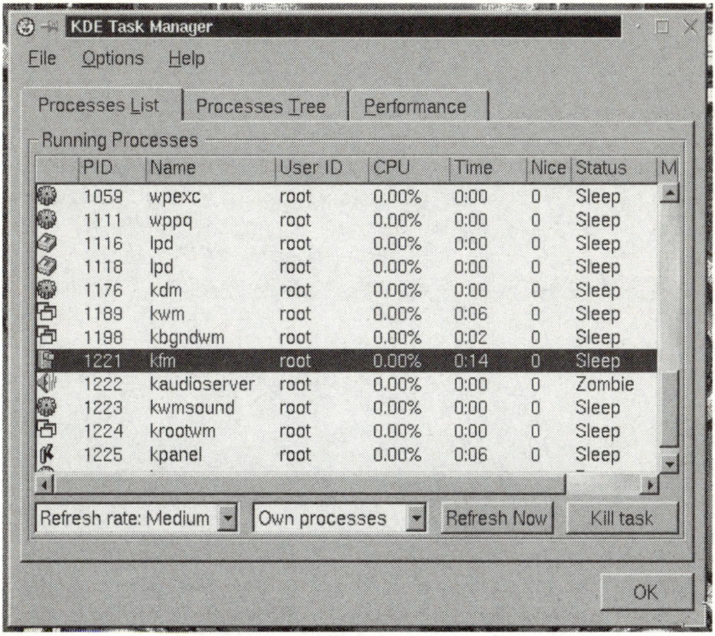

Fig.4.40 The Task Manager can be used to kill a program

must be used instead. You may find that the system is left in *ghostscript*, with a "GS" prompt instead of the usual Linux prompt. Simply use the Control-c key combination to exit to the Linux prompt. For brief help on the *ghostscript* utility, including a list of the supported output devices, use this command:

gs —help

Some of the "devices" are actually graphics file formats, but a useful range of printers is supported.

Kill

Linux is generally very stable, but no operating system can guarantee to be totally reliable since the applications software and the hardware can not be guaranteed flawless. If it proves to be impossible to halt a program via normal means there is an alternative in the form of the *kill* command from the console. Killing off the right task is something less than

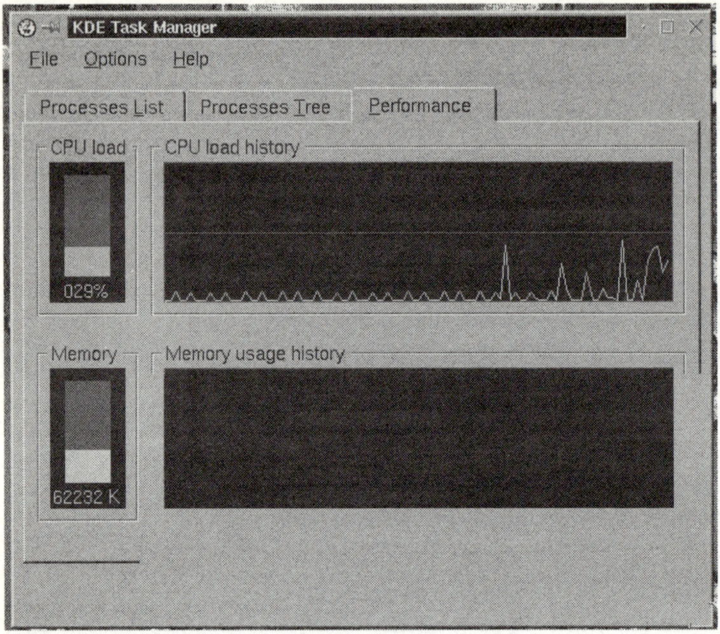

Fig.4.41 CPU and memory monitoring via the Task Manager

straightforward using this method, but the KDE Task Manager makes things much easier. Selecting System and then Task Manager from the "K" menu runs this utility. The main window area shows a list of all the tasks current running (Figure 4.40). This includes the name of the file used to start each task, so it is easy to locate the right one and terminate it using the Kill Task button. The Task Manager is the Linux equivalent of the Windows 95/98 Close Program window that is brought up by pressing Control-Alt-Delete. Like the Close Program window it should only be used as a last resort and not as the normal way of terminating programs. Another factor in common with its Windows counterpart is that it shows the background processes, and not just the programs that are in open windows. You will therefore find numerous processes that you probably had not realised were running.

If the Processes Tree tab is operated the window changes to show the running tasks in tree form, but the program otherwise functions as before. The Performance tab switches to a completely different window that enables the CPU loading and memory to be monitored (Figure 4.41).

Finally

If you have followed the story so far you will not be an expert on Linux, but you should be able to install this operating system on a PC and use it to good effect. You should also be able to install and run applications, check that you are not running out of hard disc space, copy files, tailor the KDE desktop to suit your requirements, format floppy discs, and do all the other essential tasks that you can (almost) do with your eyes shut when using Windows. It is worth looking around the menu system in KDE where there are numerous "extras" to be found. Exactly what is available tends to vary from one version and distribution of Linux to another, but there will usually be one or two joke programs such as Xeyes, which is a pair of eyes that follow the pointer around the screen (Figure 4.42). They go cross-eyed if you position the pointer between them! Right-click on one of the eyes and select Close in order to switch off this program.

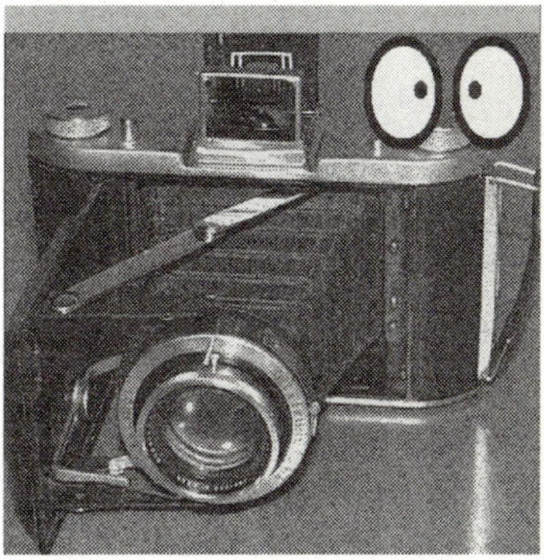

Fig.4.42 Cross-eyed Xeyes!

There are plenty of tools for configuring KDE, and it has not been possible to describe all of them in this book. Altering the wallpaper was covered in this chapter, but if you activate the "K" menu and then select Settings and Desktop there are several further options available that enable things such as colours (Figure 4.43) and the fonts to be altered. These mostly work in standard Windows fashion or something very close to it, and are easy to set up. There

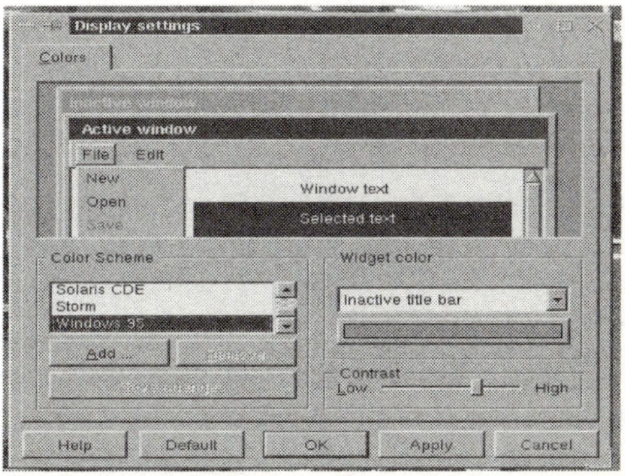

Fig.4.43 Setting the desktop colour scheme

are further options available from the Settings part of the “K” menu, and you might be able to do some “fine tuning” here. There are graphics programs available, such as the Snapshot program that was used to produce the screen dumps for this book, and drawing/editing programs such as *xv*, and Gimp. You will probably find a vector drawing program such as Tgif as well.

Fig.4.44 The KDE CD player

A typical Linux installation seems to include a few dozen utility programs. There should be an organiser, a CD player (Figure 4.44), a calculator or two, a world clock, and all the usual utilities. It is well worth taking some time to explore the menus to see if you can find some useful freebies.

Recap

View or change permissions

Right-click on the file or folder icon in KFM, select Properties and then left-click on the Permissions tab.

Show permissions (command line)

Use the *ls* command with the “-l” option.

Add a group (command line)

Use “groupadd -g IDnumber groupname”

Format a floppy disc

Activate the “K” menu, and then select Utilities and KFloppy. Choose the required disc size and format and then left-click on the Format button.

Change the wallpaper

Activate the “K” menu and then select Settings, Desktop, and Background. Click away merrily to select the required background design, colour scheme, etc., and left-click on the OK button when you have finished. Left-clicking on the Apply button enables your settings to be seen on the full display without exiting the Display Settings window.

Add/remove desktops

Activate the "K" menu, select Panel and then Configure. Left-click on the Desktops tab and the use the upper slider to select two, four, six, or eight desktops. Left-click on OK to apply the changes and exit.

Change the Panel position

Activate the "K" menu, select Panel and then Configure. Select the required size, position, etc., using the radio buttons and then left-click on the OK button to apply the changes and exit. You can left-click on the Apply button to try out new settings without closing the configuration window.

Add an icon to Panel

Find the program using KFM and drag it to the Panel. Alternatively, select Panel and Add Program from the "K" menu, and then select the required program from the menus.

Remove an icon from Panel

Right-click on the icon and select Remove.

Move an icon on Panel

Right-click on the icon, select Move, move it to the new position and then left-click.

Change the Panel size

Select Panel and Configure from the "K" menu. Then select "Tiny", Nornal", or "Large" from the radio buttons. Operate the Apply button to see the changes without exiting the configuration window.

Make an icon

Choose Graphics and then Icon Editor from the "K" menu. Draw your icon and save it with a xpm extension and save in /opt/kde/share/icons/ You can also use this program to edit existing icons.

Install a RPM package

Find the RPM file using KFM and then left-click on it. Select the appropriate options from the window that appears.

Uninstall a package

Select Utilities and Kpackage from the "K" menu. Locate the package you wish to remove in the tree structure and then left-click on the Uninstall button.

Unzip a MS/DOS zip file

Use "unzip filename" at the command line.

Read a zipped text file

In KFM left-click on the file containing the text file. In the Archiver window that then opens left-click on the entry for the text file. The contents of the file will then be displayed in a Kedit window.

Check the free memory

Use the *free* command at the command line. Alternatively, select Settings, Information, and memory from the "K" menu.

Check the free disc space

Use the *df* command at the command line.

Print a file

A file that has a suitable format for the printer can be printed by selecting Utilities and Printer Queue from the "K" menu. Then drag the file from KFM to the main Printer Queue window.

Print a file (command Line)

Use the copy command to copy the file to the mount point of the printer (e.g. "cp Afile /dev/lp0"). The file must be in a suitable format for the printer.

Print a PostScript file

It is possible to print a PostScript file to many non-PostScript printers using the *ghostscript* program, as in this example which prints "Afile":

gs -sDEVICE=epson -sOutputFile=/dev/lp0 Afile.ps

To "print" to a file the command takes this form:

gs -sDEVICE=epson -sOutputFile=PrintFileName Afile.ps

Monitor CPU and memory use

Select System and Task Manager from the “K” menu, and then operate the Performance tab.

Terminate a troublesome program

Select System and Task Manager from the “K” menu. Highlight the troublesome program in the list of tasks and then left-click on the Kill Task button. This method should not be used as the normal way of terminating a program. It should only be used when the program is otherwise uncontrollable.

Appendix 1

Useful Web addresses

http://www.linux.org.uk	Main UK and European Linux site
http://www.linux.org	The Linux Organisation site
http://www.li.org	Linux international site
http://www.calderasystems.com	Caldera Systems site
http://www.redhat.com	Red Hat site
http:/www.suse.de	SuSE site
http://www.cdrom.com	Slackware site
http://www.debian.org	Debian site
http:/www.eit.de	Easy Linux site
http:/www.download.com	General PC download site with Linux section

As one would expect for an operating system having its origins in the Internet, there are countless other sites that can be easily located using one of the normal search engines. The sites given above also have links to numerous Linux related sites.

Appendix 2

Commands to remember

Command	Description
cal	print a calendar for current month
cd	change directory
cp	copy a file
date	print the current date and time
dir	list files and folders
df	show how much disc space is free
du	show disc usage information
free	display memory information
ls	list files and folders
ls —color	list files using different colours for each type
ls -a	list all files (including hidden files)
ls -s	list files and their size
ls -t	list files in time order (newest first)
mkdir	make directory
mount	mount a device such as a disc drive
mv	move a file or folder
mvdir	move a directory
passwd	set or change a password
pwd	print the name of the current directory
rm	remove a file
rm -R	remove folder and its contents
rmdir	remove a directory
umount	unmount a device such as a disc drive

Appendix 3

Ghostscript printer support

A wide range of printers are supported using *ghostscript*, which can be used to convert the PostScript output of many Linux programs to suit these non-PostScript printers. The *ghostscript* program should be usable with these popular printers, plus many others. The on-disc documentation supplied with *ghostscript* should give up-to-date information on the supported devices. Note that some standard graphics formats are also catered for.

Canon BubbleJet BJ10e, BJ200, BJC600, and BJC800

Canon LBP811

Epson 9-pin dot matrix series

Epson 24-pin dot matrix series

HP DeskJet, DeskJet Plus, and DeskJet 500

HP DeskJet 500C series

HP DeskJet 1200

HP LaserJet, LaserJet Plus, LaserJet II, Laserjet III, LaserJet 4, etc.

HP PaintJet, PaintJet XL

IBM Jetprinter

IBM Proprinter

It should also be possible to use any printer that is fully compatible with one of the above, or has an appropriate emulation mode. Any HP DeskJet, LaserJet, or compatible that has a DOS printing mode should work with *ghostscript*.

Appendix 4

History in *bash*

In order to bring up the last command used in *bash* press the *up* cursor key. The command can then be edited using the *left* and *right* cursor key plus the Delete and Backspace keys. Press Return to execute the modified command string. There is also a sort of command line equivalent to to a Windows history palette. Use this command to produce a command history:

fc -l

You can use flags to list only certain commands in the history list, as in these examples:

fc -l -6	Lists the last six commands
fc -l 99 107	List commands 99 to 107

These keyboard codes can be used to execute previous commands:

Code	**Effect**
!	Begin substitution
!!	Repeat last command
!N	Repeat command number N
!-N	Repeat the command N number of commands back
!String	Repeat the most recent command starting with String
!N String	Repeat command N and append String
!?String?	Repeat the most recent command that contains String

Appendix 5

KDE route map

These are the routes to various KDE applications and utilities via the "K" menu.

System

KFM - (Super User Mode)

System - File Manager (Super User Mode) - then supply password

Task Manager

System - Task Manager

Desktop Pager

System - Desktop Pager

XMan (the X Windows on-line manual)

System - XMan - Manual Page

Settings

Wallpaper settings

Settings - Desktop - Background

Desktop colour settings

Settings - Desktop - Colors

Screensaver settings

Settings - Desktop - Screensaver

Active desktop borders

Settings - Desktop - Borders

Desktop fonts (including size adjustment)

Settings - Desktop - Fonts

Mouse settings

Settings - Input Devices - Mouse

Keyboard settings

Settings Input Devices - Keyboard

Memory Information

Settings - Information - Memory

Processor information

Settings - Information - Processor

Disc partition information

Settings - Information - Partitions

Panel settings

Settings - Applications - Panel

KFM settings

Settings - Applications - File Manager

Programs And Miscellaneous

Add a program to Panel

Panel - Add Application - choose the program from menu structure

Text editor

Applications - Text Editor

Advanced text editor

Applications - Advanced Text Editor

Organiser

Applications - Organiser

Screen grabber

Graphics - Snapshot

Icon editor

Graphics - Icon Editor

Kfloppy

Utilities - Kfloppy

Archiver

Utilities - Archiver

Kpackage

Utilities - Kpackage

Terminal (console)

Utilities - Konsole or Utilities - Terminal

Printer Queue

Utilities - Printer Queue

CD player

Multimedia - CD Player

Media player

Multimedia - Media Player

Index

Notes

Notes

Notes

Notes

Notes